BOOKED UP!

How to Write, Publish and Promote a Book to Grow Your Business

By Stephanie Chandler

Olympus
VN-702PC
Voice Recorder

45 00

Booked Up! How to Write, Publish and Promote a Book to Grow Your Business

By Stephanie Chandler

1. Business & Economics : Marketing - General 2. Business & Economics : Small Business - General 3. Business & Economics : Entrepreneurship

ISBN: 978-1-9359530-4-3

Printed in the United States of America

Authority Publishing

11230 Gold Express Dr. #310-413

Gold River, CA 95670

800-877-1097

www.AuthorityPublishing.com

Table of Contents

THE PATH TO PUBLISHING

When I published my first book in 2005, my goal was simply to write a book that I wanted to read. I saw a need in the marketplace and I went to work. I had no idea what kinds of opportunities I was about to unleash.

The journey began while attending a sales conference in Las Vegas in 2002. I worked in enterprise software sales, had a $4 million annual quota, and my clients were major Dot Com companies. I had reaped the rewards of the Dot Com Boom, and managed to survive the Dot Com Bust, but the only joy I found in my work came in the form of an inflated paycheck. The Silicon Valley lifestyle allowed me to pay cash for a sporty new convertible and purchase my first home when I was just 27 years old. But there is no such thing as easy money.

Our entire sales team were required to attend quarterly sales conferences, events that I grew to dread. One year I quietly had a birthday while at a ski resort in Lake Tahoe (which nobody acknowledged). I watched George Bush win the presidential race from a bar in a casino (I had to send in an absentee ballot). I plastered on a fake smile and muddled through countless off-site events, designed to teach us how to sell bigger, better, and faster.

During a life-changing conference in 2002, I was hosting a guest—an executive from a major Dot Com company, and my best client. He was also my favorite client and someone I had grown to like as a friend, so having him there was a rare pleasure in an otherwise miserable experience. We enjoyed an extravagant dinner and afterward he wanted to play blackjack. I followed him into the casino and sat down at a $25-per-hand table.

We ordered cocktails, I took two sips from mine while looking at my cards, and the next thing I knew, I hit the floor. Yep, I fainted on the floor of a casino. Seriously, if you need medical attention, it will come faster in a casino than anywhere else in the world. There were at least a dozen casino staff and medics standing over me as I tried to assess what was happening.

Someone summoned the VP of my division, who quickly appeared and announced he had a limo outside ready to take me to the hospital. As just another example of the ridiculous ways we did things, I couldn't believe that I was offered a limo instead of an ambulance ride. It seemed absurd.

I ultimately elected not to go to the hospital, and instead returned to my room. But thanks to that incident, I finally saw a doctor. I hadn't felt well for several months. In fact, I had been toting a bottle of Maalox in my briefcase and would actually take swigs from the bottle before walking into meetings. I learned that I had an ulcer, which was irritated by the stress and had caused my already low blood pressure to drop at the blackjack table that fateful evening.

It was just a few months before my 30th birthday and that event was a wake-up call. I hated what I was doing and the paychecks no longer seemed worth it. It was time to figure out how to escape the golden handcuffs.

I spent weeks trying to figure out what I wanted to do. I kept coming back to my childhood dream of being a writer. Since I had no idea how to make a living as a writer, I decided to do what I thought was the next best thing: I would open a bookstore and write novels from the office in the back.

I spent a year planning my departure and crafted a 42-page business plan. I studied every book I could get my hands on. I sent e-mails to store owners all over the country asking for advice. I did not take my decision lightly, and squirreled away money to fund my first year of entrepreneurial life.

Nearly everyone thought I had lost my mind. My corporate bosses were nothing short of shocked when I gave notice. They offered some ridiculous perks as incentive to change my mind. Knowing their tricks well, I made sure I had signed a commercial lease before I gave notice. I wanted to ensure that there was no turning back.

And off I went. In 2003, I opened a 2800-square-foot bookstore in Sacramento, California. It had plenty of space in the back for writing that novel that I knew would be coming soon. But during the process of starting that business, many people said to me, "I wish I had the courage to do what you did." They were bound by the shackles of corporate America, paychecks and family obligations. They were afraid to take the entrepreneurial leap. Their plight inspired me.

At the same time, I had begun numerous feeble attempts to write fiction, and failed miserably. I wasn't used to failure. Until then, everything I had set my mind to I had been able to accomplish.

While pondering my future as a novelist, I thought about all those business start-up books I had read and how they hadn't fully prepared me for the journey. None of them offered advice for things like negotiating a commercial lease (my sales skills came in handy here as I was able to get six months of free rent that first year!). There was a need for a more comprehensive start-up guide, something that offered free online resources and a realistic step-by-step approach. This revelation led to my first book: *The Business Startup Checklist and Planning Guide: Seize Your Entrepreneurial Dreams!*

Naïve about the publishing process, I signed up to attend the San Francisco Writers' Conference in 2005. The event featured "Speed Dating with Agents," where attendees had the opportunity to pitch books to literary agents in hopes of landing a book deal. As the only business book author at a conference loaded with writers of fiction and memoirs, I stood out in the crowd. Nearly every agent I met asked me to follow-up and send a formal book proposal. I was elated.

But then the rejections came, one by one. They all said the same thing: "You don't have a platform." One day, I received a call on my cell phone from Mike Larsen, the founder of the San Francisco Writers' Conference and a renowned agent to some of my favorite authors, including Jay Conrad Levinson.

"I like your work," he told me, "But you don't have a platform." When I asked him what he meant by platform, he said, "You need to have a built-in audience. You need to be out speaking to tens of thousands of people. Big publishers want authors to come to them with a ready-made audience of book buyers."

I pointed out that what he was suggesting was like putting the cart before the horse. "Won't I be invited to speak once I have a book to my credit?" I asked. His response? Sure, but that was my problem to solve. There was nothing he could do for me until I had a platform.

I am forever indebted to Mike Larsen for inspiring what happened next.

Since I had left the rat race behind and I wasn't in any hurry to start traveling and living a frantic life, I decided that the quickest way to build a platform would be to find an audience through the Internet. Once again, I saw a need in the marketplace. I had visited dozens of business start-up websites, but none offered free industry-specific information. In response, I launched www. BusinessInfoGuide.com, a directory of resources for entrepreneurs.

I was figuring it all out as I went along. I loaded up the site with lists of resources and began writing articles, something I enjoyed immensely. I sent my first newsletter out to a whopping eight subscribers. Today the newsletter goes out to thousands.

Since my manuscript was finished and I was impatient with the publishing process, I decided to self-publish. I had the book professionally edited and designed and released it in September 2005. The biggest surprise of all came from the website. I listed the book for pre-sale on BusinessInfoGuide.com and began receiving orders a *full two months before it was in print*.

It was at that moment that I understood what Mike Larsen meant by platform. I had found an audience eager to buy my book.

Since the site was building traffic and gaining momentum and I had more information to share, I decided I wanted to venture into selling e-books and special reports. I looked for a book on how to do this, but there wasn't one available. So I studied how others were selling information and formed my own plan. My first electronic report began selling the very first day I made it available for sale.

Can you guess what happened next?

I saw an opportunity to write a book that hadn't yet been written—the book I wanted to read (this has become a theme with all of my subsequent books). I got to work on the outline and wrote a book proposal. I sent the proposal to two publishers, and a month later received an offer from John Wiley and Sons. They were impressed by my Internet presence and in December 2006, *From Entrepreneur to Infopreneur: Make Money with Books, eBooks and Information Products* was released into major distribution.

I remember the first time I saw my book on a shelf at Barnes and Noble. It was a surreal experience, as if I was seeing someone else's success. I still get a charge out of seeing my books in a store, and I'm pretty certain that I always will.

Following the book, I ended up signing on with an agent: Andrea Hurst. We had met at the writers' conference back in 2004 and had managed to keep in touch. Since I had developed a platform, she was convinced she could help me land future book deals.

While having lunch one day to discuss my business book ideas, I handed

Andrea a copy of a workbook that I was selling through my website called *Online Marketing for Authors*. I thought that her authors might benefit from some of the information. She flipped through it while I rattled on about book ideas and then she interrupted me, "I think I can sell this." It hadn't even occurred to me to seek a book deal for that project—it was simply something I had created as a passive revenue stream.

Several weeks later, we accepted an offer from Quill Driver Books. They changed the title and released the book in May 2008: *The Author's Guide to Building an Online Platform: Leveraging the Internet to Sell More Books*. My next book, which Andrea sold to Career Press several months later, was released in September 2009: *LEAP! 101 Ways to Grow Your Business*. I was able to leverage my author status to get some incredibly fun interviews for *LEAP!* from folks like Seth Godin, Jay Conrad Levinson, David Allen, David Meerman Scott, Michael Port and many others.

How My Books Have Affected My Business

About six weeks after opening the bookstore, I realized I had made a big mistake. I hated everything about owning a retail business. I hated the hours, managing the staff, the responsibility—all of it. The only part I enjoyed was marketing and finding new ways to bring in customers. I studied search engine optimization (SEO) and quickly landed the store website into the top three results on Google. I enjoyed hosting author book signings and charitable events. Otherwise, I was never there. I put a staff in place and disappeared to write my books and build BusinessInfoGuide.com. I eventually sold the store in 2007 and my biggest regret was that I didn't sell it sooner. I had been checked out for a long time.

In the meantime, my books were bringing all kinds of opportunities. I was invited to speak at various events. I got media coverage in numerous business journals, BusinessWeek, Inc.com, *Entrepreneur, More Magazine, Wells Fargo Small Business*, Sunrise 7 (Australia's version of the Today Show) and many other media outlets.

I was also receiving e-mail and calls from readers who wanted to know about my services—services related to the books I had written. They wanted help with their business plans, with publishing their e-books, with publishing their books, Internet marketing, and the list goes on. I offered some consulting and training classes, but finally realized I was missing out on some major business opportunities.

In 2008, I launched Authority Publishing, in direct response to the needs of my readers (www.AuthorityPublishing.com). Having been through the self-publishing process, I knew the pros and cons. I also understood the path to traditional publishing, the pros and cons of that route, and how a book can be a valuable business tool.

I saw a need for a company that served the nonfiction market, comprised largely of business professionals. There are so many custom publishing companies operating as "Author Factories," churning out books in exchange for a check, yet never empowering the authors with marketing skills and knowledge. And nobody was addressing the needs of business professionals who wanted to expand their own opportunities. Authority Publishing would take a different approach, blending the benefits of publishing books in print and in electronic formats, while emphasizing internet marketing, content marketing and business growth opportunities.

As I write this, it has been just seven years since my departure from corporate America. I have since built and sold one business, published four books, created dozens of information products, written countless articles, delivered dozens of speaking engagements, and launched a company that aligns with my experiences and values.

My books have carved a path that I never expected. I often say that my path found me. For the most part, I have simply listened to my gut instincts, listened to the feedback I have received, and have been willing to embrace new experiences. It has been a spectacular journey and in many ways, I feel like it has only just begun.

This book is intended to help you discover the powers that nonfiction books offer as a tool for your business. Perhaps your book will enhance your current business or it will take on a life of its own and lead you to bigger and better opportunities. The possibilities are truly unlimited and I encourage you to be open to all of them.

Part One:
Publishing Benefits and Money-Making Opportunities

"I take the view, and always have, that if you cannot say what you are going to say in twenty minutes you ought to go away and write a book about it."

Lord Brabazon

GROW YOUR BUSINESS BY PUBLISHING A BOOK

No matter what kind of business you are in, there is no better way to become an instant *authority* in your field than by publishing a book. Better than any business card, brochure, advertisement, website or blog, a book is a powerful tool that can open doors and lead to tremendous business growth opportunities.

Think of your book as an entry point into your business. When a reader enjoys your book, he or she is going to want to know more about you. If a reader finds value inside its pages, he/she will naturally be interested in visiting your website, blog and other resources that you have available (including products and services).

When we read a good book, we become bonded to the author. We feel a personal connection, as if we know the author (or would like to). It's a natural tool for building alliances, creating fans and increasing revenues.

Still not convinced? Here are some additional reasons why business owners who are authors have the leading edge:

Increased Credibility

Writing a book demonstrates your expertise in your subject matter. It is a form of mastery that can elevate your status in the eyes of your potential clients, peers, the media, and many other key contacts. The potential is truly unlimited.

Recently, I was shopping at a local store and began chatting with the owner. When he asked what I did, I told him I own a marketing and publishing company. I never even mentioned that I am an author. Next, he asked for my card, which has pictures of my books on the back side. "You wrote these books?" he asked, with his eyes wide. "I'm going to look at your website today. I need to hire you!"

This happens all the time. When people learn that you are an author, they pay attention. Without even mentioning any specific services, the store owner quickly decided that I must be the authority he has been looking for.

Sharpen Your Competitive Edge

We all face competition and if you want to crush yours, a book can get the job done quickly. Think about it from the consumer point of view. Let's say that you want to hire a personal trainer. You interview a trainer with typical credentials. He's friendly, says the right things, and his price is typical in the industry.

Then you interview a second trainer. He is also friendly and says the right things. At the end of your meeting he hands you a copy of his book, "The Healthy, Wealthy and Happy for Life Program." It has an appealing cover design and he even autographs it for you.

Who are you most likely going to hire?

There is nothing like a book to impress prospects and close deals. Give away books like you hand out business cards and your business is sure to grow. Often, simply adding your book to your business card can be just as effective.

Earn Higher Fees

If you are a service provider, such as a consultant, coach, graphic artist, doctor, therapist, financial advisor or other business professional, your book gives you a license to charge higher rates. It all comes back to that credibility factor. You are not just an average expert in your field, you are a *published authority*. Of course your rates are higher than everyone else's.

The idea of raising rates makes some people uncomfortable. The reality is that as an author, people are going to expect your rates to be higher than the rest. If you've written a book and yet you remain the low price leader in your industry, it doesn't quite add up. You are an author! An authority in your field! If you wanted to hire Jack Canfield to coach you on success, would you expect to pay him $50 per hour? Heck no! You would pay a premium rate because he's an expert who must be in highdemand.

The other challenge in raising prices is the fear that you will lose business. And the reality is that you may lose some clients (though if you're truly demonstrating value, this becomes less of an issue). Keep in mind that when your rates are higher it takes fewer clients to earn the same income. Ideally, your income should increase as your author status drives up demand for your services.

Capture Hard-to-Get Appointments

Want to speak with the CEO, head of Human Resources, a political leader or some other unreachable contact? Send a copy of your book along with a personal note. Odds are much better that your next call will go through. "This is Annie Author calling..."

We've all heard of gimmicks in the sales world. One of my favorite examples that I heard several years ago was when a salesperson sent his prospect a VCR with a video inside (the VCR is a good indicator of how old this trick is!). He stuck a note on top that said, "Play me." The package was bulky, which made it more likely to get opened than a sales letter shoved in an envelope. Even the most guarded administrative assistant with strict gate-keeping orders is bound to inform her boss that a VCR arrived in mail! Though it was a creative idea that actually worked for that salesperson, it was also an expensive gamble to send a package like that.

With a book, your hard costs are the book itself (which you should be able to purchase from your publisher for just a few dollars) and postage. So even if it cost you a grand total of $10 to send the package, ask yourself how much this kind of marketing is worth to you. If you reel in the business of a prestigious client that you wouldn't otherwise have had, the return on investment is HUGE. I'm not suggesting that you send books out in the same volume you would send a direct mail campaign, though some authors do. But sending out books is a solid strategy for making important new contacts with the potential to pay-off *big time*.

When sending out copies cold, it is wise to follow-up with the recipient. Send a short e-mail asking if he/she received your package. I personally receive a lot of unsolicited books, primarily from authors seeking endorsements of some kind. The ones that get my attention have several qualities in common:

- ✓ The book arrives with a personal note from the author.

    The author gets bonus points if the note indicates that he/she has read or benefited from my books, blog, website, etc. That instantly creates a bond between us and inspires me to want to help.

✓ The book is somehow related to my industry.

Children's books and pizza cookbooks are nice, but they have nothing to do with my business or expertise. It would make no sense for me to endorse them. However, if an author wants to pitch me on her personal chef services and sends me her cookbook, now she's got my attention!

✓ The book is professionally produced. I don't care if it is self-published as long as it looks like a book I would find on a bookstore shelf. It should be professionally edited with an impressive cover design and quality binding.

Someone once sent me a "book" bound like a booklet from Kinkos. I love booklets; they can be great promotional tools. But sorry, you can't call it a book. Aside from that, the production quality was beyond poor. Images were hand-drawn by someone who clearly wasn't an artist. She would have been better served to use some basic clip art—and called it what it was: a booklet!

✓ The author sends a follow-up e-mail within a couple of weeks of the package arriving. Again, here the author is attempting to make a personal connection with me (not sending me some form letter that is clearly going out to tons of people). Receiving a brief, friendly e-mail is a gentle nudge that is easy for me to respond to.

Generate Referrals

Word of mouth is arguably one of the best kinds of marketing on the planet. When someone recommends a product or service, we buy. Whether that recommendation comes from a friend, a business associate, a magazine article or a television show, consumers are influenced by the opinions of others.

A good book is going to naturally generate referrals from readers. I know that when I read a book that affects my life in some way, I can't wait to tell people about it. If your book is doing its job and leading people back to your website, it will inevitably create a referral pipeline for your business.

Another way to generate referrals with your book is to introduce it to people who are influential in your industry. Several years ago, a family law attorney sent copies of her parenting book to marriage therapists all over town. Since therapists were often talking to her potential clients—people headed for divorce—she took a chance that the book might make an impression. Her law practice quickly became the largest of its kind in her city.

A side note here is that her book had nothing to do with law or her law practice. It was a parenting guide, a topic that was indirectly related to her business. Regardless, she found a way to generate referrals by sharing a good book with influential people who could send business her way. For some businesses, it takes just a few good referral sources to grow a company quickly. A book gives you the opportunity to multiply those referral sources in a big way.

Capture Media Attention

Open any newspaper or magazine and notice how each article includes quotes and advice from experts. Most often, these quotes come from authors. Tune in to any talk radio show, The Today Show, or even your local news programs. Authors are constantly in the spotlight. In fact, media professionals from print, radio and television frequently search Amazon.com for authors of books related to their needed subject matter.

Leveraging your author status means that you are a prime source for media. Your website and blog should reflect your expertise and showcase your ability to serve as a source for the media. Most importantly, you don't have to wait for the media to find you (though it's nice when they do). Reporters and producers are always looking for timely, interesting stories and expert sources who can add commentary on the topic at hand. *They need expert sources as much as we need them.*

The strategy that has worked best for me over the years is to simply send an e-mail directly to reporters. A couple of years ago, I came across an article online that was interesting and related to what I do. The journalist's e-mail address was readily available so I spent two minutes sending her a note that complimented her article. I added that I was a small business marketing expert and available for interviews if she ever needed a source. She sent me a quick thank you message and said she was adding me to her database.

Several months later, that same journalist contacted me twice in one week and quoted me in the *Los Angeles Times* business section and *BusinessWeek*. It took two minutes of my time to make that connection. The media loves to work with authors.

Also remember that if you prove yourself as a good source, reporters will come back to you again. Know your talking points, answer their questions swiftly, and follow-up afterward with a thank you note. This is a phenomenal way to remain in the reporter's good graces. I have developed professional relationships with numerous reporters who reach out to me year after year for quotes. One even calls me regularly in search of story ideas and referrals to interview sources.

Stand Out at Trade Shows

If you host a booth at trade shows, your booth won't be ordinary once you showcase your book and your work as an author. Prospects and potential alliance partners will be eager to meet the author.

To increase exposure, have a sign that reads "Author Book Signing" and offer to autograph any books that you sell (or give away). Even if book sales aren't your primary goal, it is highly likely that you will capture attention. Attendees will ask questions about your book and ultimately about your business.

You can also use your book as a prize for a drawing that you host. If you've got a budget, you could give away copies of your book to interested parties.

Get Known Online

If you want to develop celebrity status and build a following of fans, there is no faster or more effective way to do that then by showcasing your author platform online. Share tips and resources through your website, blog and social networking sites like Facebook, Twitter and LinkedIn. Host teleseminars, distribute podcasts and promote videos on YouTube. Be a guest on Internet radio programs and other people's teleseminars. The Internet is an ideal place to capitalize on your author status and reach a global audience. See the marketing section of this book for more ideas.

Generate Passive Income from Information Products

As you build a following of loyal readers, selling information products can become a lucrative passive income stream. Information products include e-books, special reports, workbooks, audio recordings, teleseminars, and virtually any way that you can compile and sell information. Information products are often quicker and easier to produce than a book, and they can perfectly complement your efforts as an author.

Perhaps one of the greatest advantages of info products is that once they are created and the distribution process is automated, they can sell around the clock with minimal effort.

Giveaways are another fantastic use for info products. For example, you can reward new subscribers to your electronic newsletter by giving away an e-book or special report. Or you could send your e-book to other business owners and allow them to distribute it for free, provided all of your contact information is included. This strategy will ultimately bring you new customers and that all-important exposure to your audience.

Here are some tips for developing product ideas:

- ✓ Conduct a survey with your customers and ask them what information they need or would like to know. Use the results to form new product ideas.
- ✓ Teach people how to do something.
- ✓ Create a directory. Do you have a list of 50 or more resources that people in your industry need? Sell it!
- ✓ Develop a companion workbook that complements your book.
- ✓ Offer training via a teleseminar series.
- ✓ Produce a video of a demonstration, speech, or technique.

Incidentally, I wrote a whole book on this topic: *From Entrepreneur to Infopreneur: Make Money with Books, eBooks and Information Products.*

Develop Programs that Support Your Book

If you don't already have programs that support the theories in your book, you may want to make them available. Whether you ask them to or not, readers will call, write and send e-mail inquiring about how to implement the strategies in your book. Consider developing coaching programs, training packages, consulting services and other services that complement your subject matter.

Build a Team Around Your Brand

You can use your book as the foundation to teach others your system for doing what you do. You could even develop your own certification program and recruit agents who deliver services under your brand, while they also promote your book and generate revenue for your business.

For examples, check out the following:

- ✓ Jay Conrad Levinson's "Guerrilla Marketing Master Training" program: www.gmarketing.com
- ✓ Jim Horan's Consulting Team: www.onepagebusinessplan.com
- ✓ Michael Port's "Book Yourself Solid Certified Coach" program www.michaelport.com

This is a fascinating and potentially lucrative business model. The authors listed above have each built a brand around their books. They offer certification programs and provide training for others to teach their systems. Did I mention that their candidates pay thousands of dollars to go through the certification training? And once certified, these folks become marketing agents as they pound the pavement promoting the books and the related brand. Simply brilliant, don't you think?

Schedule Speaking Engagements

If you want to grow your business and reach a lot of people quickly, consider developing your skills as a professional speaker. There are dozens of trade organizations in every major city that need speakers for their weekly or monthly meetings. You can leverage the instant credibility that comes with being an author and use your book as a door-opener for speaking opportunities.

Start by offering to speak for free to gain experience, then convert to speaking for a fee. Professional speakers earn a wide range of fees ranging from $500 to $10,000 and up for top keynote speakers. And even if you never charged a speaking fee, when done right, these engagements can generate plenty of revenue opportunities from new clients and back-of-the-room sales.

You might be surprised by how quickly your business can grow as a result of your speaking engagements. Soon, you may find that you don't have to go looking for speaking opportunities. As you build a reputation and reach the masses, the invitations to speak will come to you.

Become an Instructor

Authors are welcomed as instructors at adult learning programs like the Learning Annex and many colleges. These organizations will promote your classes through their catalogs and direct mail campaigns and that publicity can bring great exposure and new business opportunities. In fact, back when I was negotiating my first book deal, I was also teaching periodic classes through The Learning Annex and Learning Exchange. The publisher pointed out that this was a plus since these venues send catalogs out to tens of thousands of people. Talk about awesome exposure.

Hold Your Own Events

Authors like Jack Canfield, Tony Robbins, Robert Kiyosaki and countless others leverage their notoriety and experience to host their own revenue-generating events and workshops. Events can range from half-day meetings in a rented office space to week-long events at a hotel or even on a cruise ship.

For some, holding annual events can be the biggest revenue-generator of the year, surpassing revenues from all other business activities.

Sell Large Quantities

Identify the target audience for your book and look for opportunities to land bulk sales agreements. For example, a trade association could purchase and give away copies of your book to new members. A corporation could use your book as training material or as a give-away at its annual conference. A non-profit group might be able to use your book as a promotional tool or even a revenue-generator by purchasing quantities from you at a discount and selling individual copies at full price. A bank might want to offer your book as a bonus for those opening new business accounts.

Consider the types of organizations that could benefit from your book— whether they are comprised of your target audience or they are also marketing to your target audience. Offer deep discounts on bulk orders and create a win-win situation.

Build Buzz

A couple of years ago, a friend who was the president of a local chapter of Business Networking International (BNI) showed me a book he had received in the mail. Along with the book was a letter from the author letting him know that the book was provided with his compliments (and most likely sent to hundreds of people in similar roles).

What a smart idea! The author sent complimentary copies of his book to leaders close to his target audience. The goal was to build a buzz and get people talking about the book. It clearly worked since my friend was anxious to show it to me, and I suspect, he also shared it at his BNI chapter meeting.

FREE!

Chris Anderson, author of several books including *The Long Tail: Why the Future of Business is Selling Less of More*, launched an interesting campaign to promote the release of his new book *Free: The Future of a Radical Price*. He made the book available for free in e-book format and in audio on Audible. com (and last time I looked, it was still available for free download and well worth the listen). What did this radical offer do? Inspire people to talk about it (like I'm doing here), which leads to book sales, consulting gigs, speaking engagements, etc.

Seth Godin is also a fan of free give-aways to promote his books. Whether giving away the e-book version or a bonus with purchase, he is a master of building buzz with the concept of FREE.

If your goal is to generate business with your book, giving away the e-book version costs you nothing, yet can yield big rewards. However, know that it's unlikely a traditional publishing company will allow you to do this unless you manage to negotiate it into your book deal contract (the publisher gets the majority of the rights—a frustrating down side). But if you self-publish, the control is yours and you give it away as much as you want.

Uncover Opportunities You Didn't Even Know About

Over the years, I have launched a variety of services, including a publishing company, as a result of listening to readers of my books. I pay attention to what kinds of questions readers are asking and how I can solve their problems.

There is a good chance that writing a book is going to help you uncover new revenue opportunities. That may mean that you develop new consulting programs, workshops, workbooks, e-books, or even a series of future books. Welcome feedback from your readers because it reflects their needs and gives you an opportunity to address them.

INTERVIEW PROFILE

Name: Jim Horan
Business Name: The One Page Business Plan Company
Website: www.OnePageBusinessPlan.com
Book Titles:

- The One Page Business Plan for the Creative Entrepreneur

- The One Page Business Plan for Non-Profit Organizations

- The One Page Business Plan for the Professional Consultant

- The One Page Business Plan for Financial Services

How did your journey as an author begin?

I (just barely) graduated from San Jose State in 1974 with a Bachelors degree in business administration and accounting. I got Cs in English.

While working as a consultant, I was meeting with an avant-garde architect. Next to his table was a chart pad. It had "Xs" and "Os" on it and was very cryptic. He said, "This is my one page business plan."

I started to play with the idea of what would go with a one-page plan. I realized that people speak in keywords and short phrases. When I would meet with a client, I would jot down their keywords and phrases and within about 90 minutes, I had their plan.

Back then I was in a wonderful support group: The Bay Area Entrepreneurs Association. I went to my group and told them I was working on this one page business plan idea. They asked me to give a presentation and afterward they told me that I needed to get out and do some public speaking. I told them that I don't do public speaking and they said, "Well, get over it."

In my own One Page Business Plan, I decided to do four presentations in the coming year (1994). I did five. The next year I did 15-16. Audiences began asking for a book. So I went back to my entrepreneurs' group and asked them what I should do; I told them that I didn't know how to write a book. They told me once again, "Get over it. Go write a book."

I found the Bay Area Independent Publishers Association (BAIPA), a wonderful organization, and attended their one day self-publishing university. I also read books by Dan Poynter and John Kremer.

I started and stopped writing the book about half a dozen times. Then I met Rebecca Salome. She's a book coach who helps people get their books written. It took three years to write and publish, but I finally finished.

Not long after the book came out, I had requests from clients in corporate America for software. So I went back to my entrepreneurs' group and asked what to do. They said, "You're going to need to create software. Go figure it out!"

I had a client who was in the early stages of developing Web software. The product came to market June 1, 2000.

How did your subsequent books come about?

Along the way, consultants began to gang up on me. They were all doing volunteer work with non-profits who needed help with their plans. I told them I would write the book if they would help me. They submitted sample plans and that's how we ended up with *The One Page Business Plan for Non-Profit Organizations*.

Then, for the 10th anniversary of my first book, I decided to celebrate at Confab, the annual conference for the Institute of Management Consultants (IMC). We gave all 300 people there a copy of the book as our way of saying thank you for all that they had done to help me learn how to be a successful consultant.

A few months later, the CEO of GAMA (General Agents Management Association) called. He said, "These plans are amazing. This industry needs them. I'll do everything I can to help you put a book together for them." And that turned into *The One Page Business Plan for Financial Services*.

Every time we add another book to our series, it increases sales across the board. People who didn't know about our books before suddenly get introduced to them.

Have you had any other surprises along the way?

About five years ago, I got an inquiry from Korea to buy the foreign rights to my book. My sense told me that I might only get one check from them ever, so I better make it big. They paid $5,000.

Then I connected with Bob Erdmann, a foreign rights specialist. He sold rights to McMillan in India and Wiley in the UK. We also sold rights to publishers in Mexico, Estonia and Vietnam. One reason every author should consider offering foreign rights is that the buyer has a vested interest in protecting your book from getting reproduced illegally.

After we sold rights to Mexico for $650, we asked if they were planning to produce an 8x11 version—all of our books are 8x11—but they were producing the book in a smaller size. They didn't want to print the larger version so we asked if they would sell the translated version back to us. They did—for $650—and we recently released the new Spanish version here in the U.S.

Since you're a self-publisher, do you have a distributor to place your book in bookstores?

No, I don't bother. We have arrangements with Baker and Taylor and Ingram (book distribution portals), though their sales are minor. Amazon is a big percentage of our sales. Our consultants also order from us and about 40 to 50 college professors do too.

Did you pursue the college market?

No, it just kind of happened. That's the magic of books. When you take what you know and do it to be in service of people, they will buy your book and talk about it.

What kind of marketing have you done for your books?

I built my own indirect sales force of 450 consultants.

I wanted to find people who were already trusted advisors to my audience. For those people, they would be *sharing* information about The One Page

Business Plan, rather than *selling*. Business consultants were already working with clients whose business plans weren't working. So we created a training and certification program. Nine years later, over 450 consultants have been through our program.

By the way, the consultants pay us to get certified. Back then we charged about $2,000 for the program. Today we charge $4,800 for four half-day training programs, all delivered by teleconference. They don't have to travel and this keeps costs down for all involved.

We teach them how to extract a One Page Business Plan from anybody and how to know when a plan is done. It should represent your best thinking. That's the litmus test.

When we sit down with clients to review their plan, we can see that it looks pretty good, but we're not experts in their industry. So we ask, "Does this represent your best thinking?" If the answer is "no," then they're not done with their plan.

How much speaking do you do now?

In the early years I was speaking 30 to 40 times per year. Now, maybe 12 to 15 times. I'm more selective.

What have been the biggest surprises about how your book has affected your business?

I didn't know that I could write a book and I didn't know that people would think differently about me.

When I'm out in the business world, instead of introducing myself as a consultant, I introduce myself as an author. Something about this intrigues people. What I didn't realize, and have come to learn, is that an author is still revered in the world. For people who are consultants, I tell them that they all need to write books.

There was no way I could have possibly known all of the beautiful things that happen when you write a book. I never could have imagined that I'd be a public speaker, author, selling thousands of books and bringing awareness to corporate America.

In Washington, D.C., a senior executive at Oracle bought my book on Amazon. He went back and bought 90 copies and began requiring his direct reports to use the process. Today, over 1,000 Oracle sales reps, managers and executives use The One Page Business Plan model.

Have you received any media exposure as a result of your book?

The book has been featured in *Oprah Magazine*, *Entrepreneur*, *Money*, and things like that.

Do you have any advice for others?

One of the things I talk about when I go out and speak to people who are out of work is that instead of looking for a job, go look for a way to *work for the rest of your life as you are.* If you keep moving towards that which you are attracted to, you'll figure out the details along the way.

You can have a dream, but what are you going to do with your two feet? You need to move forward. Just keep moving in the direction that you're attracted to. Leverage your talents. Few people find writing easy, but you can get good at it.

Part Two:
Self-Publishing and Traditional Publishing Demystified

"The best way to become acquainted with a subject is to write a book about it."

Benjamin Disraeli

THE PUBLISHING DECISION:
TRADITIONAL VS. SELF-PUBLISHING

The world of publishing can be broad and complex because the options and rules are constantly changing. I have personally made it a point to pursue both self-publishing and traditional publishing and will continue to leverage both for their distinct pros and cons. Here are some to consider:

Self-Publishing Pros

- ✓ You keep control over all of your rights.

- ✓ Individual book cost is low, resulting in a higher profit margin when you sell books yourself.

- ✓ Distribution is available on Amazon and other online bookstores, making it easier than ever to reach a broad audience since the majority of us are buying books online anyway.

Self-Publishing Cons

- ✓ You have to do all the work: establish a publishing company, purchase an ISBN, get the cover created, lay out the text, get listed with distributors, etc. (unless you hire a custom publisher for assistance).

- ✓ Startup costs can be high since you typically have to purchase a large quantity of books if you do it all yourself, or invest in custom publishing services.

- ✓ Revisions can be expensive if you haven't yet sold the bulk of your initial inventory (beware of ordering more books than you can sell).

Traditional Publisher Pros

- ✓ Added credibility when your book is published with a major press—for some organizations, this makes a difference.

- ✓ Broader distribution is more likely available vs. publishing yourself.

- ✓ Your book is likely to appear on bookstore shelves (though it will be pulled quickly if the book doesn't sell and the majority of consumers buy books online).

Traditional Publisher Cons

- ✓ Unless you make the best seller list or leverage your book to grow your business, you aren't likely get rich. Publishers typically pay authors around $1.50 per book sold!

- ✓ Book advance checks are lower than ever: averaging around $5,000 to $10,000—and you must earn that back, $1.50 at a time, before you will see any additional royalties.

- ✓ You will lose control and many of the rights to your work. For example, most publishers require exclusive rights to the e-book version of your book, meaning that you can't sell or distribute it to anyone.

How to Land a Book Deal

If you read the introduction of this book, you learned about platform. Publishers want authors of nonfiction books to come to the table with a platform—an audience of buyers for the book. If you are a speaking, reaching tens of thousands of people, if you have a high-traffic website or blog, if you write a column or have some other type of celebrity status, your odds of landing a deal will be dramatically increased. The harsh reality is that without a platform, it is much harder to land a book deal.

With that in mind, here's the process for getting started:

- ✓ Write a query letter. This is a compelling description of your book and why you are the best person to write it.

- ✓ Research publishers and agents. Some small and mid-size publishers will accept author pitches directly, while larger publishers like Random House will only work with agents.

- ✓ The best way to find publishers that specialize in your genre is to investigate other books in the same category. Find out who is publishing related books and visit each publisher's website to locate Submission Guidelines.

- ✓ For agents, a good place to start looking is the Association of Authors' Representatives: www.aaronline.org. Members are agents who are bound by a strict code of ethics. A literary agent should not require any payment to work with you. Agents work like brokers and leverage their contacts and connections to place books with publishers. On average, they receive 15% of a book contract, including 15% of royalties and advance. While this may sound steep, it can be worthwhile if you find an agent with the right connections and who knows how to negotiate a book deal. I navigated my first book deal on my own, and those contracts are long and mystifying. It is a relief to now have an agent who has my best interests in mind and who knows what points are most negotiable.

- ✓ After researching websites for submission guidelines, you can begin sending your query letter to agents and/or publishers. Keep in mind that it is probably going to be a numbers game. The more letters you send, the more you increase your chances of getting some attention.

Many big name authors, including Stephen King and Jack Canfield, received dozens of rejections before landing a deal.

✓ The goal is to receive a request to send additional information. For nonfiction books, most publishers and agents want to see a book proposal, an outline and at least two sample chapters from the book. (The next section covers elements of a proposal.)

✓ Some good news: Your book manuscript doesn't need to be completed before you begin to pursue a traditional publisher! For nonfiction books, an outline and sample chapters will do. When you are offered a contract, you can negotiate the time needed to complete the writing process.

✓ After sending a proposal, you basically have to sit back and wait. Most don't want to receive follow-up calls, though some will encourage you to send an e-mail to follow-up on a submission. Check the website for guidelines and stick to them. Sending gifts, cards, flowers or singing telegrams is not the way to succeed at this game.

✓ Pay attention to the feedback you receive. If you get responses that indicate your book has already been done before, re-craft your pitch to showcase how your book is different or better than the competition.

✓ Start an "Acceptances" folder. When I was going through this process, I quickly filled up a "Rejections" folder. I decided to create an "Acceptances" folder and eventually I received my first one. It was a shift in mindset that kept me focused.

✓ Pay dirt comes when you are offered a deal. Your head will spin in circles and you will want to celebrate—and you should! But don't lose sight of the realities of the contract. If you don't have an agent, it would be wise to hire a literary attorney or other professional to help you understand and negotiate terms. Like any business transaction, there are many points to be negotiated and revisions that need to be made. You may regret accepting what is offered at face value.

A Few Publishing Realities

✓ It typically takes a traditional publisher a year to complete your book and put it into distribution. With the amount of red tape they have going on, the process seems to take forever. Just don't expect to see your book on shelves within a few months, as this is highly unlikely.

✓ You will be involved in the editing process and asked to turn it all around quickly. You may or may not like the proposed changes and you may or may not have a voice in the ultimate outcome.

✓ Cover design is another point where you will probably have little input. The publisher will design something and may send it to you for review, but requests for changes are unlikely to be met.

✓ Don't expect an impressive level of marketing. Most publishers don't have big marketing budgets, and therefore leave the bulk of responsibility to the author. You might appear in their catalog, in a press release, and may get featured at a trade show, but don't count on them landing you an appearance alongside Matt Lauer. Those efforts are reserved for established, big-name authors. My books are placed with three traditional publishers and combined, these folks have scored me ONE radio interview and a handful of reviews in obscure publications. Disappointing, to say the least.

✓ Once you release a book with a traditional publisher, they will have first right of refusal on your next book (a major contract detail). This means that you can't release a subsequent self-published title or pursue another book contract without first being turned down by your existing publisher. If you want out of your contract, I recommend pitching them something you know they won't want.

✓ I personally choose to pursue a combination of traditional and self-publishing. I like the notoriety and exposure that comes with my traditional book deals, though I resent the lack of control and pitiful compensation. With my self-published titles, I make more money per book and maintain control. These options can complement each other nicely.

✓ If you are unable to land a traditional book deal, then self-publishing can be a great option. Many self-published authors have gone on to land future book deals so if this is a goal for you, just be patient and continue building your platform and appeal with the publishing industry in mind. It is a myth that self-publishing kills your chances of landing a traditional contract. If you are able to demonstrate success with your self-published title by selling more than 1,000 copies or so, it will only increase your appeal with the powers that be.

✓ Sometimes traditional publishers seek out self-published authors. I know several authors who have been approached by the "big dogs," which can demonstrate an interesting shift in power. In one case, an author who writes books for the firefighting industry quickly turned down a rather substantial offer. He simply makes too much money on his books to give it all away. He also didn't want to give up control and has built his own distribution channels so that his books are devoured by his target market. The publisher didn't relent and instead returned with an even bigger offer. He turned that one down too.

HOW TO WRITE A BOOK PROPOSAL

A good book proposal should be convincing, fully edited for spelling and grammatical errors, and thorough. Keep in mind that your proposal reflects you and your professionalism so you want to make sure it is high-quality and follows industry standards. Proposals can range from 10-50 pages.

A proposal should have the following elements:

✓ Typed on 8.5 x 11 white standard bond paper.

✓ Contents should be double-spaced.

✓ A footer should indicate the author's name and book title.

✓ Pages are numbered consecutively.

✓ A standard font, such as Times New Roman, in 12-point size for easy reading.

✓ Should not be stapled or bound with anything other than a large binder clip.

Book Proposal Outline

✓ **Cover Page** – This should include the book title, sub-title, author name, estimated word count for the final book (typically 60,000 words or more), and author's contact information (address, phone number, e-mail address and website URL).

✓ **Overview** – Two to five pages that highlight the most important elements of the book. Keep in mind that your first few paragraphs are your best chance to hook the agent or editor. If these aren't engaging, the rest of your proposal may not be read. Explain why the world needs this book, what the book is about, and why you are the best person to write it. If you are able to obtain any endorsements from celebrities or well-known authors, list them.

✓ **Market Analysis** – One or two pages that explain who your target readers are. Indicate any recent supporting statistics that demonstrate there is an eager audience.

✓ **Competitive Analysis** – List at least five books that would compete with your title. Write a couple of paragraphs for each, explaining the strengths and weaknesses and how your book will be different or better. Make sure to cite the author, publisher, and date of publication for each book.

✓ **Promotion Plan** – Two or more pages that describe how you will market this book. This is quite possibly the important element of your proposal so put a lot of thought and substance in this section. List any media experience and contacts that you have. Indicate if you write articles for magazines or if you regularly perform any type of public speaking.

Keep in mind that most publishers don't spend much to promote new authors. You can offer to do a book tour, but you will most likely have to fund the tour yourself. If you have a significant amount of money that you plan to contribute to promotion efforts, indicate this here by saying, "The author is willing to match the publisher's promotion budget up to $xx.xx." If you plan to spend less than $10,000, leave this statement out. They are looking for a substantial commitment and credibility.

✓ **Chapter Outline** – Include chapter titles and key points for each chapter. This can be a bulleted list or several paragraphs describing each chapter.

✓ **Author Bio** – Give a brief overview of your qualifications, previous writing credits, and anything that will justify why you are a good person to write this book. This is not the place to list your hobbies, pets, or other irrelevant details. Stick to the topic at hand and demonstrate your authority on the subject. Most importantly, if you have a large following (huge mailing list, regular speaking engagements, etc.), make sure you repeat it here.

✓ **Delivery Information** – This is a short paragraph that lists the estimated word count of the completed manuscript, the number of months needed to complete the manuscript, and how the manuscript can be delivered (via a Word document on disk is preferable).

✓ **Sample Chapters** – Include two or three sample chapters. These do not necessarily need to be concurrent so you might include chapters one, three and ten if they are your best work and are ready to go.

✓ **Supporting Documentation** – Include copies of published articles, publicity materials, and anything that demonstrates your talents, accomplishments, and promotional abilities.

Resources for Writing a Book Proposal

✓ How to Write a Book Proposal by Michael Larsen

✓ Write the Perfect Book Proposal: 10 Proposals That Sold and Why by Jeff Herman and Deborah M. Adams

THE SELF-PUBLISHING JOURNEY

Self-publishing provides a wonderful opportunity for any author who wants to take control over the publishing process and get their words into print. But because self-publishing is so easy to accomplish with a few bucks and some typed pages, many authors make mistakes along the way.

As a former bookstore owner, I have seen it all. A steady stream of authors used to parade through the store with their books and I could instantly tell when a book was self-published on a budget. From low-quality cover design and lack of editing to unreasonable pricing and an absent marketing plan, at least 90% of the authors I encountered made some major mistakes.

You can avoid new author pitfalls by preparing to be successful. Following are some guidelines to get you started on your journey.

Quality Matters

I cannot emphasize this point enough: *Successful self-publishing starts by producing a book that looks like it is hot off the press from a major publisher*. The cover should be professionally designed and the text should be thoroughly edited by a pro—not your spouse, friend or business partner. Your book is a reflection of you. It should be impressive from start to finish. Cutting corners with design and editing will surely be reflected in book sales and potentially on the results you hope to produce for your business.

Avoid rushing through this process or cutting corners. Ideally you should hire a designer who is experienced with book covers and an experienced editor who has worked on books. While cheap labor may be in abundance, you usually get what you pay for.

Pricing Considerations

Some of the print on demand (POD) companies force authors to set unreasonable prices for their books. A standard bookstore will expect to purchase your book at 40% off of the retail price and Amazon.com takes a whopping 55% discount. The price for your book should be reasonable for your target audience, yet still leave room for you to make a profit.

For example, if your book has a retail price of $20, a bookstore will purchase it at 40% off, which comes to $12. In order for you to make a profit, you should be able to purchase wholesale copies of your book for less than $12. Unfortunately, some publishers lure authors in with low set-up fees, but make up for it in higher per-book costs.

Conversely, I have seen 100-page trade paperbacks with a retail price of $25 or higher. Unless the subject matter is highly technical or specialized in an industry that can bear this kind of pricing, it will be difficult to convince consumers to pay such a high price for a short book. When researching custom publishers, be sure to inquire about the purchase cost of your books and how the retail price will be set.

Placing Your First Order for Books

When researching the minimum order requirements of book publishers or printers, consider how many books you need. Your purchase price for books will always be lower when you order in large quantities because printing costs are reduced. However, if you order thousands of copies, you will need a climate-controlled place to store them and a plan for selling them.

I advise authors to order enough books for one year. This means that you must tabulate how many you can realistically sell. If you are a professional speaker and can pre-sell books to companies and associations, you may be able to commit to several thousand copies. If your plan is to slowly distribute books one at a time, it probably doesn't make sense to order thousands.

Make a list of potential sales opportunities and how many you think you can sell over the course of a year. Also, if you're serious about marketing your book, plan to send out at least 100 review copies to media professionals. Book reviews sell books and authors should be willing to give books away in order to gain valuable publicity. One mention in a local newspaper can translate into a flurry of book sales. Expand your reach to online media, bloggers, radio show hosts, television and trade journals and you will uncover plenty of opportunities.

Marketing Begins BEFORE You Publish

One of the biggest mistakes an author can make is to wait until a book is in print to begin the promotion process. There are literally hundreds of book marketing strategies that you can begin to tackle right away. See the marketing section of this book for more ideas.

> *"If you don't have the time to read,*
> *you don't have the time or the tools to write."*
>
> Stephen King

STEPS TO SELF-PUBLISHING

Self-Publishing Checklist
Form a publishing company.
Establish a form of ownership (sole proprietor, partnership, corporation, etc.).
Apply for business licenses and permits through your county offices.
Purchase an ISBN (visit www.Bowker.com).
Obtain a barcode (a list of providers is available at www.isbn.org/standards/home/isbn/us/).
Copyright your work (visit www.copyright.gov).
Register with the Library of Congress (visit pcn.loc.gov).
Hire a professional cover designer.
Write excellent sales copy for the back of your book cover.
Hire an editor to make sure your copy is pristine (do NOT skip this step!).
Hire an interior layout specialist.
Research book printers and request quotes for printing. Beware of printing more books than you need—they will end up taking over your garage, basement, spare bedroom, etc. You might also decide to update your book long before you sell out of your inventory.
Set a profitable price for your book. Most bookstores require a 40% - 55% discount off of retail. Make sure your price leaves room to make a profit while offsetting printing costs and still coming in at a marketable rate.
Get your book listed for sale through Amazon.com and other online merchants.
Locate a book distributor for major distribution.

Shameless Self-Promotion

Many new authors find that the work involved in truly self-publishing a book is simply more than they want to tackle. This is why custom publishing has become a booming industry. If you want to fast-track the production and distribution of your book, consider working with a custom publisher (such as www.AuthorityPublishing.com!).

INTERVIEW PROFILE

Your Name: Whitney Roberts
Business Name: The Bar Code
Website: www.thebarcode.net
Book Titles:

- *The Bar Code Cheat Sheets (in Action)*, 2005 (1st edition), 2008 (3rd edition)
- The Essay Code (2009)

Synopsis of Your Book:

The Bar Code Cheat Sheets book is really nothing more than a series of essay templates that cover specific areas of law tested on the California Bar Exam. They provide the student with canned, ready-set skeletons that they can plug right in to an essay question and adapt to a given fact pattern.

The "cheat sheets" are popular because they condense massive amounts of legal material into easily-absorbable approaches for topics that are normally difficult for students to grasp and organize. The templates are presented in the exact way the subject matter will be tested—in one to four-page formats that are a breeze to manage under timed test conditions. They are also well known for the colorful anecdotes and footnotes that accompany each template, in which tips, tricks and common exam mistakes are discussed and blatantly made fun of. References to current news stories and celebrities are frequently included in order to make the reading less boring.

Since the essay component of the California Bar Exam is worth a lot of points, and often the area people struggle with the most, the book has developed somewhat of a cult following, much to my surprise. We ended up being the "little start-up that could."

Here is the description from the website (geared toward someone who already is familiar with the California Bar Exam):

The Bar Code Cheat Sheets are essay "templates" designed for the larger, more complex issues tested on the California Bar Examination. They are roadmaps or skeleton outlines that lay out in detail the organizational structure applicants should follow for a variety of selected essay topics. The Cheat Sheets offer a ready-set approach designed to minimize "thinking" and "organizing" time at the outset of each essay.

Included with each Cheat Sheet are detailed footnotes that offer tips and tricks for how to analyze each of the legal principles contained therein. The Bar Code Cheat Sheets are designed to be a supplement, not a substitute, for a complete set of substantive review materials.

The Bar Code Cheat Sheets in Action book contains a copy of each of the Cheat Sheets listed below and a sample answer that illustrates how to incorporate each Cheat Sheet into an essay for the California Bar Examination. Each answer was written by Whitney Roberts, former bar grader and founder of The Bar Code review course, and was specifically designed to show students how to write passing answers in the scoring range of 80-85 within the one-hour time limit.

Description of Your Business:

I used to offer a full service test preparation company for students studying for the California, Nevada, Arizona and New York Bar Exams. We offered private tutorials, small classes, large workshops and textbooks to help students prepare for the written components of these exams. Today, the company offers only textbooks. The classes have been either reduced to book format or are now licensed to other companies.

How has being an author has directly impacted your business?

Within a few years of its release, I was able to semi-retire thanks to the book. The great word of mouth it received in our very small, niche community, has allowed me to live off the proceeds without doing any marketing (exception: maintaining the website and shopping cart). Of course, the book never would have been successful without the students who took our courses because they were forced to USE it in conjunction with our classes. Those students started talking about it, which set the marketing wheels in motion. Eventually people who couldn't take our courses for financial reasons, or who were geographically limited from attending LIVE classes had access to our methodology from the comfort of their home.

Of course, the LIVE classes exploded in size because of the book as well. Where we used to utilize the workshops to promote and sell the book, within a few years, the book was selling out the workshops. It was an interesting and unexpected transition. Eventually, I decided to move the company in the direction of books, so that I could pursue other endeavors in different industries.

Have you received any media exposure as a result of your book?

I have had some media exposure in which the book was discussed, but I'm not sure the book was the reason I was approached. It certainly helps to give credibility to the brand and to me, as the founder.

What are some of your favorite marketing strategies for your business and your book?

We rely very heavily on word of mouth and testimonials. Time and time again, customers tell us that they decided to purchase the book after reading the testimonials on the website (many of which are incredibly detailed). Whenever someone offers to write one, I am so grateful. I never say no.

How would your business be different today if you hadn't authored a book?

It's hard to say exactly where I would be without it. I can't imagine it because the book is so much a part of my life and my journey now. I am very thankful for the friends and former students who encouraged me to write it.

Knowing what you know today, is there anything that you would do differently?

I wouldn't do anything differently, despite the fact that my approach was unusual. I self-published, I turned down 80% of the wholesale agreements I was offered, and I didn't use distributors. I flew by the seat of my pants a lot of the time. But it all worked out in the end.

Maybe I would take back the time I threw away a few hundred copies and spent thousands to reprint because I found a couple of typos. I'm not that much of a perfectionist anymore!

Do you have any advice for entrepreneurs who want to write a book?

Yes! If you find yourself being sold into the "sexy" idea of being published, think again. Authors stand to make very little money off of traditional publishing deals, and big houses don't do nearly the amount of marketing you think they will. Consider self publishing. Look into people who offer assistance in that regard. Roll the dice on yourself if you have a good product. And by all means, HAVE A GOOD PRODUCT.

What are your plans for the future?

Write. Sleep. Explore. Repeat.

AUTHOR'S NOTE: Whitney's book retails for $139.95! This is important to note since very few authors are fortunate enough to live off the proceeds of a single $15 book.

Part Three:
How to Write Your Book—FAST!

"Writing is easy. All you do is stare at a blank sheet of paper until drops of blood form on your forehead."

Gene Fowler

TARGET AUDIENCE

Before you begin to write your book you should know who you're writing it for. Knowing your audience will help you not only develop your manuscript, but identify methods for marketing your book and evaluate your total sales potential. Since you are crafting your book as a way to grow your business, your customers or alliance partners will likely be a primary consideration.

Are you writing a book for:

- ✓ Moms of toddlers?
- ✓ Teens?
- ✓ Men who are sports fanatics?
- ✓ Realtors?
- ✓ Realtors who market to the affluent?
- ✓ Independent business owners?
- ✓ Corporate executives?
- ✓ Corporate employees?
- ✓ Dog owners?
- ✓ Cat owners
- ✓ Low-income individuals?
- ✓ High-income individuals?
- ✓ Single women?
- ✓ Married women?
- ✓ Men ages 25-45?
- ✓ Retirees?

Think about your target audience and how your book can appeal to them. What do they want to know? How you can your book meet their needs? What problem does your book solve? Though your book may appeal to more than one target demographic, having a main target in mind will make all the difference.

EVALUATE YOUR COMPETITION

Once you know what you want to write about, you need to find out what other books exist on your topic. If you are pitching to a traditional publisher, this exercise is a required part of the process. But even if you are self-publishing, you should evaluate your competition so that you know how to position your book as different or better than what is already available.

The easiest way to find competing titles is to search www.Amazon.com for keywords on your topic. For example, if you want to write about how to start a consulting business, search the business books category for the following key words:

- ✓ CONSULTING
- ✓ COACHING
- ✓ ADVISOR
- ✓ START A (insert specialty such as financial planning, marketing, etc.) BUSINESS

If the market is saturated with books on your topic, consider narrowing your focus. For example, if you run a pet-sitting business, you could write a book called, *How to Start a Profitable Pet Services Business* and include chapters on pet sitting, obedience training, grooming, and dog-walking. If the market is over-saturated with books in this genre, you could change your focus to *How to Market a Pet Services Business or Real-World Advice from Pet Business Owners*.

Be sure to poll your potential audience. Ask business contacts and customers if they would be interested in reading a book like yours. Find out what kind of information they want to learn about. Study your market carefully before you proceed so you don't end up wasting your time on a book that has already been written and is well-established.

Don't be discouraged if there is already a book out there that covers your topic. Most genres have multiple guides with similar topics (self-help books are a great example—consider how many books exist on relationships!). With millions of readers in the world, there is always room for another guide as long as it takes a different approach.

GETTING YOUR BOOK OUT OF YOUR HEAD AND ON TO PAPER

The idea of starting from scratch to write a book can seem overwhelming and daunting. Following are some guidelines to help you get through the process.

1. Decide on a Topic

If you have multiple book ideas in mind, decide which has the most market appeal. You should always keep your audience in mind as you develop your book.

2. Know Your Book's Unique Value

There were over 480,000 books published in 2008 alone, so if you're worried that there is not enough room in the world for a book like yours, don't be so sure. The key is to establish how your book will be different or better than the competition. Determine what unique value you will bring to your readers.

3. Choose Your Process

You don't have to be a professionally-trained writer to develop a book. Here are several options:

- ✓ Hire a ghost writer
- ✓ Enlist a co-author
- ✓ Dictate your book on audio and use software such as Professionally Speaking© to convert it to text or have the recordings transcribed
- ✓ Get your thoughts on paper and hire a professional editor to turn it into a manuscript
- ✓ Assemble an anthology of contributions from others

4. Leverage Content You Already Have

Your book may already be further along than you realize. If you have created content for your business, you may be able to use it for your book. Here are some places to look:

- ✓ Articles and blog posts you have written
- ✓ Hand-outs you have developed
- ✓ Surveys you have conducted
- ✓ Case studies and client success stories
- ✓ Seminars, videos, and recordings you have made that can be transcribed
- ✓ Contributions from others (articles, interviews, case studies, etc.— with their permission, of course)

5. Get Started with an Outline

Everyone has their own unique process for writing, though most writers will tell you that they start with some sort of outline. I recommend using a storyboard process.

Start with a blank wall and a stack of Post-it notes. Write each and every topic idea you want to cover in your book on a Post-it and stick it to the wall. Once you have all of your ideas out, move the notes around until they form some kind of logical order. This is a great way to identify your chapters, how much content you have for each, and where you need to add more content. You can transfer everything to an outline or simply work off your wall of ideas.

6. Begin the Writing Process

Once you know what topics to cover and you have crafted an outline to chart your course, you are ready to begin writing. To make the writing process seem less overwhelming, tackle it in small pieces. When approach it bit by bit, it can begin to come together quickly. Here are some ways to manage the writing process:

✓ Approach each topic as if you were writing a short article. This will help you stay focused on the topic at hand while making it easy for your readers to enjoy.

✓ Break up the text with plenty of sub-headings and bullets. This makes for easier reading, which your readers will appreciate.

✓ Share stories (real-world or fiction examples) and use metaphors to illustrate important points.

✓ If you get stuck on a topic, move on to something else and return to it later.

✓ Avoid editing while you write—this can slow you down. Write first and edit later!

✓ Beware of getting side-tracked. If you stop the writing process to research something online, it can be easy to lose track of time. Make a note about the added work you need to do and keep writing.

✓ Develop a system for jotting down notes when you need to add more information, look up a resource or any other kind of follow up. You might mark a spot in the manuscript with "xxx" so that you can easily search and follow up later.

✓ Include quotes from people you have interviewed, provide resources for additional information, and compile brief sidebar tips to enhance the reader's experience.

✓ Pack as much value into your book as possible. The best way to gain a fan is to write a book that has impact. Don't be afraid of giving away your trade secrets. If you fear that readers won't need to hire you as a result of reading your book, think again. Though you outline the details in writing, many will want to seek help and as the author, you will be the logical first point of contact.

✓ Don't obsess about the length of your manuscript as it could affect the quality of the content you write. Focus on writing for the reader and getting the most important points across. If you need to expand your manuscript later, you can always add case studies, sidebars, statistics or other data if it makes sense. Sometimes it makes sense to keep it shorter as long as the value is included.

7. Don't Forget to Promote Your Business

Your book shouldn't read like one big sales pitch, but it should encourage the reader to visit your website for additional information. In *The Success Principles* by Jack Canfield, the author provides numerous downloads throughout the book, including an entire workbook that the reader can access for free.

The brilliance of this strategy is that not only do these downloads provide additional value, they prompt the reader to visit the website several times. Guess what happens as a result? Readers inevitably sign up for Canfield's newsletter, learn about upcoming seminars, etc.

In my own experience when writing *LEAP! 101 Ways to Grow Your Business*, the publisher set a limit on the word count for my manuscript. I wrote an entire chapter of resources I wanted to include and since there wasn't room, the book directs readers to download the chapter from my website.

8. Make Time to Write

One of the biggest excuses that aspiring authors have is a lack of time to get a book written. Like anything else in life, if you want it badly enough, you have to find a way to make it happen.

You may want to plan your writing time around when you are most creative. Are you a morning person or a night owl? Perhaps you need to get up an hour earlier or stay up an hour later. It is important to discover your own unique process. Some writers are disciplined and write during a set time each day. Some schedule one or two days each week for writing.

I used to stay up late and write almost every night. But these days, with a busy schedule and a young son, I no longer have the time or energy. To ensure I still get my writing done, I actually check in to a hotel every four to six weeks and write like a maniac! In fact, I'm currently enjoying a room at the Homewood Suites with a view of the water and a fridge filled with bottled water. It's all about what works best for you.

9. Set a Deadline

Most of us are more focused when we are working toward a deadline. This helps with achieving all kinds of goals. For your book, you might set a deadline to have your book ready in time for a conference or event you will be attending. Choose a date that has some significance—maybe the five-year anniversary of your departure from corporate America or the day you plan to give notice to leave corporate America—and post that date somewhere that you will see it daily.

10. Cross the Finish Line

The average nonfiction manuscript is around 60,000 words. Two typed pages are the equivalent of around 1,000 words. So if you wrote just two pages per day, your book would be done in 60 days!

You can also work backwards by writing toward the deadline you have set for yourself. If you are speaking at a major event in six months, and you plan to publish your book yourself prior to the event, you will want to finish your manuscript at least two months prior. That gives your four months to complete the work. If you're writing 60,000 words, then you need to write 15,000 words per month in order to meet your deadline.

Once your manuscript is complete, you will begin the editing process. I find the editing and rewrite processes are the most challenging because this is when you discover inconsistencies and items that need to be changed, removed or expanded. And if you are self-publishing, as I've said repeatedly in this book, be sure to hire an experienced editor to assist with the finishing touches. Make sure to include editing and revision work within your timeline if you are writing toward a specific goal date.

CHOOSING A BOOK TITLE

The title of your book can be almost as important as the book itself. The title is often your first opportunity to grab a potential reader's interest. It's often best to stick with a descriptive title so readers instantly know what the book is about. A bit of play-on-words is okay, as long as the theme is still obvious. You can also use a sub-title to further describe the contents. Here are some examples of catchy and descriptive titles:

- ✓ Good to Great: Why Some Companies Make the Leap and Others Don't by Jim Collins
- ✓ Patent it Yourself by David Pressman
- ✓ How to Buy, Sell, and Profit on eBay: Kick-Start Your Home Based Business in Just 30 Days by Adam Ginsburg
- ✓ Starting an Online Business for Dummies by Greg Holden

Make a list of at least ten potential titles and sub-titles. Move words around until you narrow it down to three or four options. Next, survey colleagues, friends, and family and ask for their opinions. Most importantly, check to see if the title is already in use by another author. Visit Amazon.com to search for titles and make sure yours is unique.

Another important consideration: keywords. In today's Internet-centric world, knowing what keywords a user would use to search for a book like yours can be incredibly valuable. I was strategic with the title for my first book, *The Business Startup Checklist and Planning Guide*. There was very little available when I searched Google for "business startup checklist," and nothing available on Amazon. Every year since, I have been consistently contacted by reporters in December and January who are writing articles on how to start a business for the new year. They love the checklist concept as it provides simple steps they can use to model their article by. Bottom line: keywords can have an impact.

ADDITIONAL BOOK ELEMENTS

Dedication

Some authors like to include a dedication page or write a special note of thanks to those who supported them (agent, publisher, spouse, family, friends, etc.). This is optional and is a personal choice for each author. Write your dedication or brainstorm people and topics to cover in your dedication.

Testimonials and Foreword

Every author should attempt to seek testimonials to be printed on the book jacket and inside the book. Testimonials from published authors and well-known industry experts can help add credibility to your work and make it more attractive to the media and consumers. You may also want to invite someone prominent to write a foreword for your book.

And while you may think that some big name authors are unreachable, I have news for you. Smart authors know that putting their endorsement on a book only adds to their marketing exposure. The key to getting their attention? Just ask. Approach them with confidence and vigor. Don't bore them or cause them to question their decision by explaining that this is your first book. Simply state that you are the author of XYZ book and you would be grateful for an endorsement.

Many authors don't even have time to read your entire manuscript and will give you a testimonial based on a few sample chapters and information you provide in your book overview. Let them decide how much information they want to see.

The first step is to make a list of people you would like to get testimonials from. Don't be shy! Consider your favorite authors who write in a similar genre. Authors are surprisingly accessible and many still check their own e-mail. Look for contact information on their websites. And here's a little insider tip for you: connect to your favorite authors via social media sites like Facebook and LinkedIn. You can easily send messages through these sites and if the author isn't reading his own messages, he probably has an assistant who is. Trust me, I've done this myself and it works!

You will want to write to each author personally with your request. Make your letter brief, professional, and inject some of your personality into it. It will help tremendously if you are familiar with the author's work and can mention this in your letter (flattery never hurts!).

Also know that some authors will want you to provide some sample testimonials that they can choose from. That's right: they won't even bother to write it and will instead either select yours word-for-word, or modify a few things to make it their own.

About the Author

Write a brief bio that you want to share with readers. Some authors include a paragraph, others include a page—it's up to you. Topics you may want to discuss include:

- ✓ Professional background
- ✓ Education
- ✓ Current business or profession
- ✓ Achievements or awards
- ✓ Previous publishing experience
- ✓ Personal details (family, city of residence, etc.)
- ✓ Contact information (you want readers to reach out to you, right? Include your website URL and optionally include an e-mail address and phone number.)

STEPS TO GETTING YOUR BOOK DONE

	Book Manuscript Task Checklist
	Identify a target audience for your book.
	Evaluate your competition.
	Understand what makes your book different or better than the competition. This matters more than you know—especially if you plan to pursue traditional publishers.
	Define a goal to write _____ number of words per day/week.
	Give your book a compelling title. Then ask for feedback from others. The reality is that you will probably change your title a dozen times or more before you are done writing the book!
	Make a list of research tasks that need to be completed, if applicable.
	Create an outline for the book with key points that you plan to cover.
	Write a dedication (optional).
	Solicit testimonials and foreword (foreword is optional, testimonials are not!).
	Write your author bio and get a professional photo taken. Your author photo should not be a snapshot from a family outing.
	Send sample chapters to trusted readers for reviews and feedback.
	Have your manuscript edited by a professional. Period.
	Develop your author platform.
	Decide if you will pursue a publisher or do it yourself.
	Don't give up! Evaluate all feedback you receive and make appropriate adjustments.

ACTION PLAN FOR WRITING YOUR BOOK

Use the following chart to determine how long it will take you to complete your book. Typical nonfiction book manuscripts average between 50,000 words (for a shorter book) to 80,000 words (for a much longer book).

Projected Word Count: _____

Number of Words You Plan to Write Per Week: _____

Number of Weeks to Completion: _____

Calculate by taking total word count and dividing by number of words per week. For example: 65,000 total words, writing 2,500 words per week = 26 weeks to completion. That's just 500 words per week day (one typed page!) in order to complete a book manuscript in less than six months. You can do it!

INTERVIEW PROFILE

Your Name: Karl W. Palachuk
Business Name: Great Little Book Publishing Co., Inc. and KPEnterprises
Business Consulting, Inc.
Website: www.SMBBooks.com and www.KPEnterprises.com
Book Titles:

- The Network Documentation Workbook

- Relax Focus Succeed: A Guide to Balancing Your Personal and Professional Lives and Becoming More Successful in Both

- The Network Migration Workbook

- Managed Services in a Month

- Service Agreements for SMB Consultants

Synopsis of Your Book :

The Network Documentation Workbook is workbook that describes how to fully document a computer network for SMB (small and medium sized businesses) computer networks. The book includes 100+ pages of forms with complete explanations of each.

Relax Focus Succeed® is a self-help book designed to help busy people find success by balancing their personal and professional lives – and being more successful in both. This book provides a framework for setting goals in a realistic manner and bringing consistency into the various "roles" we all play in our lives (parent, spouse, employer, community member, etc.).

All of my other books are focused on helping technical consultants be better at their jobs.

Description of Your Business:

Great Little Book Publishing Co., Inc. provides books, audio programs, and live trainings for technical consultants who want to improve their businesses. In addition to carrying all of the materials produced in-house, GLB runs a web site called SMB Books that sells other books written by and for small and medium business (SMB) consultants. SMB also carries general business titles.

KPEnterprises is a small technology consulting company in Sacramento, California. We provide technical support through a comprehensive support system called "Managed Services" and support clients with 10 to 100 desktop computers. One of our key differentiators is our commitment to staying on the cutting edge of the technologies used by small and medium businesses.

How has being an author has directly impacted your business?

There are two sides to my story. Both KPEnterprises and Great Little Book benefit from being "sister companies."

Luckily, my *Network Documentation Workbook* has been well received. We have sold thousands of copies all over the world. For the clients we focus on, there is literally no other product that provides the forms and templates necessary to document an entire computer system.

As a result, we can advertise that we "Wrote the Book" on how to properly document and maintain a computer network. In general, it gives us great credibility to small business owners.

Similarly with *Relax Focus Succeed®*, I am able to position myself as a serious business person and not just a technician. Business owners like to deal with other business owners who have some of the same problems. This book has been a great starting place for conversations.

So while I can't say that I've gained a great deal of new business because of my books, they have helped me gain credibility as an "expert" and that has led to additional work.

The other side of my story is that my first book, *The Network Documentation Workbook*, led to speaking engagements, books-for-hire, and a certain level of name familiarity within the community of SMB consultants. As a result of this, I have been able to create several additional books and e-products that are sold all over the world. From these I launched a business focused on educating technical consultants and providing books and other resources for them. I have a mailing list that exceeds 10,000 names, and my new business continues to grow very nicely, even during the recession.

Have you received any media exposure as a result of your book?

Indirectly. As part of my promotion for the books and my online store, I started blogging. Between blogging and doing in-person trainings, I have become one of the people who gets called by the trade journals from time to time. I've learned that these folks are hungry for news of any kind. So I've started collecting names of people to keep in touch with when I need a little press.

It's also great to re-broadcast any good P.R. you get. It helps the magazine or website to get new eyeballs on the page. And it helps build a community of followers who say "atta boy" and keep me informed when I get positive press that I'm not aware of.

What are some of your favorite marketing strategies for your business and your book?

My basic approach to marketing my books and business at the same time is to participate in the online community. I am very active in following key people, commenting on their activity, and engaging them. When I blog about something, I also engage them. In some cases we blog back and forth, encouraging our readers to read each others' blogs.

By participating and giving freely, I've proven myself to be part of the online community. I've prepaid my dues. So when I ask for something or post something commercial in nature, I'm seen as and insider and not an outsider. On rare occasions I will actually ask a group of bloggers to blog about a specific topic, and even give them the exact phrases to use. The response is good because they know I'll do the same for them.

And when a group of prominent bloggers all say the same thing, it can have a huge impact on visits, readership, and buyers.

How would you business be different today if you hadn't authored a book?

My technology business would not be much different, although we might have a couple fewer clients. But my book publishing and selling business would simply not exist. I have somehow managed to leverage a few books into a $250,000 online book store and training business. The entire thing goes back to one book that laid the groundwork for everything else.

Knowing what you know today, is there anything that you would do differently?

I would start blogging and building my own audience more aggressively right from the start. Early on I was lucky to have my book distributed by someone with a huge audience and a huge mailing list. Whenever he sent out an email the orders poured in. And I didn't mind paying him his fee. But when he decided to stop distributing books, I found myself with no mailing list!

Luckily I had a bit of a platform and knew some people to exchange links with, so I could start growing my mailing list. But when I found myself out on my own I think I had only 400 people on my email list. Always remember: whoever makes the sale owns the customer. My distributor made all the sales for two years and thousands of buyers went onto his mailing list instead of mine.

Do you have any advice for entrepreneurs who want to write a book?

First, just do it. You might find it difficult – or nearly impossible. But if you have an idea, get it out there!

Second, figure out how you can place yourself as an expert in some field. Engage the online community. Become a contributing member before you ask for anything. Participate. Give without asking anything. Then after you've established yourself as an active member of the community, invite them into your world of expertise.

Third, you may find it easy to blog. Some people find that they are extremely expressive on a blog even if they "can't write" under normal circumstances.

Once you get a bunch of blog posts, they can become the fodder for a book (or a second book).

Most importantly, tackle something about which you're passionate. That will show through in your writing. It will energize your blog and help you to be a leader in the online community. And all of that will lead to activities in writing, blogging, speaking, and more. And since you started with passion, it will all be extra fun for you!

What are your plans for the future?

Interestingly enough, I find myself at the stage where I need to re-write some of my books. Because I'm in the technology arena, things change very quickly. My first book is almost four years old. That's more than two computer generations!

One of my books will need a major overhaul in 2010 because of some new technology that might make the old version irrelevant. And one book needs an update so I can add information about major changes in my industry.

The bottom line: I have some re-writing to do.

At the same time, I have inked a deal to co-author a book over the next six months and need to keep that project on track. And I'm writing a completely new book on a new server technology that will be coming out this year (2010). So my company is set to product five books in 2010.

Is there anything else you would like to add?

For me the most important factor is expertise in a certain area. From that everything else follows. There are also rewards between the world of publishing and the area of expertise. For example, I have had several companies offer me discounts or even free services so they could say that I am one of their subscribers.

I probably receive discounts in the range of $30,000 per year in my technology business due to my activities in the publishing side. Note that I have never signed a deal for this or agreed to endorse or promote anything. But I certainly consider it to be a benefit from my writing!

Part Four:
Marketing on the Internet and Beyond

"If opportunity doesn't knock, build a door."

Milton Berle

LAUNCH AN AUTHOR WEBSITE

Though you can promote your book on your business website, an author website allows you the freedom to build your personal brand as an authority in your field. Use yours to build an audience, share samples of your work, list your accomplishments and impress industry professionals, clients and alliance partners. An author website is also an ideal place to promote yourself as a speaker and/or consultant. Following are pages to include:

Home Page

This should summarize who you are, what you're about, and details about your book. Remember that your site is a personal branding opportunity and should reflect your best representation of yourself.

Book Page

Your book deserves to be showcased on its own page, which you can add before the book is even finished. Talk about motivation for reaching your goals! Be sure to provide visitors with a way to purchase your book. If you are shipping books yourself, a simple shopping cart solution like one offered by Paypal.com should work just fine. If you don't intend to sell and ship your own books, provide a link where visitors can easily purchase books online (such as to Amazon.com). Also, don't forget to offer a way for visitors to pre-order your book. You should list a realistic publishing date that includes a few weeks' cushion in case there are any delays in getting your book to market.

About the Author

Here is where you can include an extended bio. This might include a story about who you are and how you got to where you are, education background, work experience, awards and honors you have received, and a professional photo. Some additional photos of you at work or at play can also work well here, provided they don't hurt your credibility but showcase your personality.

Services

If you offer consulting or other services, list them here. If you want to route people to your business website, write a brief summary of services and provide a link to the site that opens in a new window.

Speaking

If you are a speaker, or want to be a speaker, a speaker page can be a valuable asset. Here you can list your speaking topics with detailed benefits. Adding a speaker page to my site was one of the best moves I've made. I have been booked for paid speaking gigs simply because that page shows up in search engines. Those who have booked me that way were not necessarily familiar with my books, but the added credibility of my author status certainly helped in getting those engagements. You can see my page at

stephaniechandler.com/professional-speaker.htm

Media

Your media page is a place to feature any past media coverage you have received along with archived press releases, additional photos of yourself (in high resolution for print publications), an extended bio and any other details the media might need to cover you in a story. Be sure to include contact information for how you want the media to reach you.

Contact Information

I am always surprised by the lack of information provided on the contact page of websites. Here you should include a phone number, e-mail address and physical mailing address. If you are home-based, get a mailbox and use that address (never publish your home address). A mailing address provides credibility. You can also include a link to your business website if appropriate.

Additional Considerations

✓ Post articles that you've written.

✓ Provide a sample chapter from your book.

✓ Include a sign-up box for gathering e-mail addresses. Even if you don't want to send an e-newsletter, you can send periodic announcements to your mailing list. An e-mail list is golden and it should always be a priority to build your list. Offer visitors some incentive for signing up such as a bonus report or audio recording.

✓ Include links to your social media profiles in prominent real estate on your site (top half of your site, ideally in a sidebar across all pages).

✓ Learn about search engine optimization or hire someone to do this for you. Ideally, your site should include relevant keywords that your readers would use to find you. Those words should be repeated throughout the text.

✓ Update your site frequently. Not only does this help your ranking in the search engines, but it ensures that your content is fresh and relevant and it gives readers a reason to come back and discover something new.

PROMOTE WITH A BLOG

A blog is essentially an online diary that allows you to post information, tips, thoughts and ideas in a running log format for others to view. I personally believe that every author should have a blog because the benefits are so great. Here they are:

Search Engines Love Blogs: The major search engines provide higher rankings to sites that update data frequently. When you post to a blog several times each week, you content is constantly changing and growing. The search engines will reward your effort with improved search engine rankings.

Build an Audience: A good blog can attract many new customers and readers. People who like what you have to say will pay attention to your blog by subscribing to your blog feed.

Content is Archived Forever: Each post to your blog adds to your growing index of content. The more content you have, the more reasons you give the search engines to find you. For example, if you wrote a post last month about the lifespan of a blue butterfly, when someone searches the Internet for that particular subject, there is a good chance that your post will be returned in the search results (depending on the competition for the related keywords).

Establish Yourself as an Authority: Hosting a blog is one of the quickest and easiest ways to showcase your expertise in your subject matter. When you share valuable tips and resources, you engage readers while building credibility in your industry.

Get Media Exposure: The media is constantly on the hunt for sources to interview for stories. From magazine and news reporters to major radio and television producers, blogs are becoming a strategic place for the media to find talented industry experts. This has by far been one of my favorite benefits of my own blog. I have received a lot of media exposure as a result of reporters and producers stumbling across entries from my blog.

Leverage and Repurpose Blog Content: It doesn't take long to build up a substantial amount of blog content. You can repurpose your posts into articles, e-books, books and reports. Conversely, you can share all kinds of content in your blog including excerpts from your book.

How to Start Your Blog

1. Search the Internet for blogs in your industry and do a little research before you start. Studying other people's blogs will help you identify what you like and don't like and how you want yours to look and feel.

2. If you already have a website, check with your hosting provider to see if they provide a blog plug-in option. If not, popular blog services include www. Typepad.com, www.Wordpress.com and www.Blogger.com.

3. Establish several categories that appeal to your target audience. For example, my business growth blog has more than a dozen categories including articles, book recommendations, technology tips, resources for authors and online marketing. Categories make it easy for readers to browse through your past entries, and also give you more creative options for developing content.

4. Develop content ideas for your industry. Your blog can include personal opinions, book reviews, links to helpful resources, industry statistics, product recommendations, excerpts from books or white papers (for which you own the copyright) and much more.

5. Keep it simple. Blog entries do not need to be long. In fact, online readers prefer brief content that is easy to scan. I recommend writing just one to three paragraphs for each post. Use sub-headings and bullets to make the text easier to read. Photos and videos can also add visual appeal.

6. Add outgoing links to your blog posts when appropriate. For example, if you mention an article you read in XYZ magazine, make sure to include a hyperlink to the article. Not only will your readers appreciate the option to view the sites you reference, but having links pointing to other sites can further improve your search engine rankings.

7. Schedule time to work on your blog. You should be posting at least three times each week for best search engine optimization. Instead of logging in several times each week, write several blog entries at once and then schedule them to publish on specific days.

8. Promote your blog by including your blog link in your e-mail signature, on your website, in social media profiles, and anywhere else you can find to share it with the world. You can also submit it to directories such as www.

BlogCatalog.com and www.Technorati.com.

9. Consider minimizing some of the effort involved by inviting others to contribute. Your blog could include guest posts by employees, customers, peers or strategic partners.

10. Maintain your momentum. Be on the lookout for fresh topic ideas so you can avoid getting "bloggers block." When you come across something interesting, get in the habit of writing it down so you have it handy when it's time to update your blog.

It may take some time to build momentum for your blog, but in the long run, the rewards can be significant. When the call comes from a major media source or a big client referral, you will know that it was all worthwhile.

ARTICLE MARKETING ONLINE AND IN PRINT

Promoting with articles has long been one of my favorite marketing strategies. Here's how it works:

- ✓ Write a brief how-to type article about a topic of interest to your target audience.
- ✓ Include an author bio of less than a paragraph that explains who you are, includes your book title and a link to your website.
- ✓ Submit the article for publication to websites and print publications.
- ✓ Post the article on your website or blog.
- ✓ Reap the benefits. By publishing a single article to dozens of online and traditional publications, you have the ability to reach all kinds of new readers and clients for your business. Since your bio includes details about your book and website, you are bound to gain new fans. As an added bonus, posting your articles online adds links pointing back to your website. This is great for search engine optimization since Google wants to see lots of incoming links to your website.

Generating Article Ideas

Every author can find topics for articles. For example, if your book is about finding the right career, you could write articles about job hunting, effective interview skills, negotiating salaries, and dressing for success. An attorney could write articles about business law, while a leadership consultant could write business-related articles for her target audience of business executives.

Submitting to Internet Content Portals

There are dozens of content sites that allow you to post articles that others can reprint in their newsletters, websites and blogs. While you make the article available for free reprint, anyone who uses your article must provide proper credit and include your bio with website link.

You might be surprised by how quickly your articles—and your website link—will proliferate across the Internet once you begin posting to content sites. For years I have made it a steady habit to write one to two articles each month and then have my assistant submit them to my favorite content portals. Here are some of the top content sites:

- ✓ www.ideamarketers.com
- ✓ www.ezinearticles.com
- ✓ www.articlecity.com
- ✓ www.goarticles.com
- ✓ www.scribd.com

Submitting to Websites

Many websites operate on a limited budget and appreciate high-quality articles written by authors. Ideally you want to offer your articles for reprint to websites that reach your target audience. The best way to accomplish this is to begin searching for sites on Google and build your own contact list. Each site should offer submission guidelines and if you can't find them, contact the site administrator or owner to inquire. You can simply submit your articles for consideration or offer to swap articles with website owners and co-promote each other.

Submitting to Print Publications

Publishing articles in newspapers, trade newsletters and magazines can be an excellent way to attract a new audience of book readers. Many smaller publications will reprint your article along with your bio and website link. Even though you may not be directly promoting your book in your article, readers will visit your site or investigate your book if they like what you have to say.

Trade magazines and neighborhood newspapers are an excellent place to start since they are often in need of writers. Consumer magazines can also be a source for your articles, although the popular magazines that you find on the checkout stands of grocery stores are the most difficult to break in to. It is best to start with smaller or regional publications.

To get started, visit your local bookstore to find smaller magazines or conduct searches on Google. You can also search sites like www.newspapers.com, or newsdirectory.com. Locate contact information for the editor in the publication masthead or website. Many websites offer writer's guidelines where the editor will indicate whether she accepts submissions via e-mail and what kinds of articles the publication accepts. The most important item to note here is that you are submitting an article for reprint. The larger publications rarely accept reprints and in the journalism world, this is an important distinction.

Use the following format to submit your articles:

Resumes That Rock
By Edna Entrepreneur
Word count: 975

<insert article body>

<insert author bio>

*This article may be reprinted provided the author bio is included. Thank you very much for your consideration.

Edna Entrepreneur
<insert contact information>

LEVERAGE PODCASTS, INTERNET RADIO AND TELESEMINARS

As an author, one of my favorite book promotion strategies is to serve as a guest on online podcasts, teleseminars and Internet radio shows. Though I have done my share of traditional radio interviews, online interviews have many advantages:

✓ The show host will promote you to their networks prior to the show. Many promote interview announcements on numerous sites across the Internet.

✓ The shows are often archived online for years, giving you ongoing promotion value.

✓ Many post the podcasts for their shows on iTunes.

✓ You get far more time online. A traditional radio show might have you on for five to fifteen minutes. An online show will often make you the primary guest for up to a full hour.

✓ Because many online listeners are sitting at a computer, they are more likely to visit your website or purchase your book right away. Listeners in a car have to jot down your information and remember it later.

✓ Online show hosts are always in need of guests so the opportunities are abundant.

To become a guest on an online teleseminar, podcast or Internet radio program, start by putting together a brief pitch. Mention your credentials (I am an author/expert/consultant/speaker/etc.) and one to three suggested topics that you can cover. Highlight a few benefits of your discussion in a bulleted list and then send it to hosts and ask if they would be interested in having you as a guest.

Tips for locating interview opportunities:

✓ Search the Internet for keywords related your target audience plus "teleseminar," "radio," or "podcast."

✓ Check sites like www.BlogTalkRadio.com, www.wsradio.com and www.airamerica.com to find relevant programs.

✓ Search podcasts on iTunes and visit the host's website.

✓ Search for events on online directories to find teleseminars that would be a good fit for you. Some directories to check are www.EventBrite.com, www.PlanetTeleclass.com and www.SeminarAnnouncer.com.

✓ Always be on the lookout for opportunities. And remember that if you're building an online platform as an expert, eventually these opportunities will start to find you!

Once you are invited to be a guest, provide the host with a media sheet. This should include a brief bio about you, your professional photo, an image of your book, and contact information. Most importantly, include a list of ten to twelve sample questions for the host. Most media professionals love these and may interview you directly from your list. Whether they use your questions or not, they will appreciate your professionalism.

Lastly, be sure to thank the host after every interview. Take the time to send a personal note. This is a great way to not only show your gratitude, but to be remembered and invited back in the future.

HOST YOUR OWN TELESEMINARS

Hosting teleseminars can have all kinds of benefits. You can offer free teleseminars as a way to build your mailing list—participants must register for the event in order to receive access. You can also conduct educational teleseminars and charge a fee. A training series spread out over several weeks can be an appealing offer. And if you invite guests to be featured on your teleseminar, you have an awesome opportunity to reach out to and connect with some influential people.

Here's how to get started:

1. Decide on a topic and how you plan to deliver it. Will it be a Q&A with a guest, will someone interview you or will you be the sole speaker leading in lecture format?

2. Write a compelling title and description of the event.

3. Sign up for a service such as www.FreeConference.com, www. GoToMeeting.com or www.InstantTeleseminar.com. You will pay a minor fee to record the calls.

4. Create an account with www.EventBrite.com. This service allows you to manage event registrations. There is no charge to process free events and they charge a small transaction fee for paid events.

5. Promote your event in as many places as possible. Here are some to include:

    Create an event on Facebook

    Post on the Wall of any social networking groups that you belong to on Facebook, LinkedIn, etc.

    Announce your new event via Twitter, Facebook, etc.

    Post to www.Craigslist.org for several cities.

    Post to sites such as www.SelfGrowth.com, www.SeminarAnnouncer. com, www.Events.org.

    Also post to any other sites where your target audience is located. This can include newsletters, message boards, classifieds, paid ads and any place that can bring exposure for your event.

6. Be sure to create a script for your event so that you have a strong

opening and closing message and enough content in between. Consider how you want to address the audience. Allowing questions at any time can disrupt the flow of the call. I recommend muting the line during the presentation and then opening up the line for questions a few times during the call.

SOLICIT SUPPORT FROM FAMILY AND FRIENDS

When it comes to book promotion, it is important to use all of the resources at your disposal. Your family, friends and peers are ideal candidates to help you spread the word about your book. Send them an e-mail that details specific ways that they can help. Here is a sample message:

Greetings!
My new book <title> is now available and I would be grateful if you can help me spread the word. Here are some ways you can assist:

- ✓ *Send a book announcement to your friends and contacts who might be interested in the subject matter.*

- ✓ *Place a link to my website from your website or blog.*

- ✓ *Visit my blog and post a comment on any of my posts.*

- ✓ *Publish a book announcement in your newsletter, trade publication or website.*

- ✓ *Help me build my social media platform by connecting with me on Twitter <insert profile link>, Facebook <insert profile link> and LinkedIn <insert profile link>.*

- ✓ *Buy my book! <insert link to purchase>*

I am also looking for some additional contacts to help me promote the book. Who do you know? Here are contacts I am seeking:

- ✓ *I will be speaking on the topic of <insert topic> at trade associations, colleges, and events that reach my target audience of <insert audience>. If you know anyone who can assist with booking me as a speaker, please let me know.*

- ✓ *Online media is also an important focus. If you know anyone with an influential blog, website, online radio show or related platform, I would love to be connected with them.*

- ✓ *I have several articles available for reprint. If you or someone you know has a newsletter, website or other publication that would be appropriate for my articles, they can be accessed on my site: <insert link>.*

✓ *Who else do you know who might be able to assist? I am open to all ideas so please send them to me.*

Thank you very much for your support,
<your name>

"A person who publishes a book appears willfully in public with his pants down."

Edna St. Vincent Millay

BREAK INTO SPEAKING

If you want to grow your business, sell more books and reach a lot of people quickly, consider developing your skills as a professional speaker. There are dozens of trade organizations in every major city that need speakers for their weekly or monthly meetings. As a featured speaker, you receive instant credibility and establish yourself as an expert in your field. Your event (and you!) will also be promoted to the entire membership of the organization, even if only a fraction of the members attend.

Be sure to think outside the box. Your presentation can be loosely related to your book, as long as it addresses the needs of your audience. For example:

- ✓ A financial advisor could present "Managing Small Business Cash Flow"

- ✓ A Web designer could present "10 Ways to Make Your Small Business Look Big"

- ✓ A life coach could present "Effective Strategies to Build Business Relationships"

In addition to trade associations, consider teaching at your local adult learning centers and community education programs. Even if only ten students register for your class, your business is promoted in their catalog, which is often sent to tens of thousands of people. Other potential venues include retirement centers, community centers, churches and charitable organizations.

Here are the steps to getting on the speaking circuit:

1. Write a brief and interesting description of your presentation and what attendees will learn.

2. Contact local trade associations *that reach your target audience* and let them know that you are available to speak.

3. Pack your presentation with useful information. *Do not make it a sales pitch for your business or book!* If the audience likes what you have to say, they will want to learn more about you and your business.

4. Your presentation doesn't need to be formal. Write an outline for your

own reference and keep it with you while presenting so you stay on track.

5. Engage the audience by asking questions and soliciting their participation.

6. Use props for visual interest.

7. Give attendees something to keep such as a single page hand-out with tips or a booklet. Be sure to include your contact information.

8. Respect the time allotted. It's better to finish early than late—then you can open the floor for questions.

9. Wrap up with a brief pitch for your book or your business and let them know you will be available for questions after the presentation.

10. Send the event coordinator a thank you note!

Make sure to have your book available for sales at the back of the room, along with other marketing materials and hand-outs to promote your business. Most organizations are happy to provide you with a display table and the ability to promote your products and services. You can also provide the audience with a special offer. For example, "Save 30% off a consultation when you schedule one with me today!"

While you will initially begin speaking for free as a way to gain exposure and experience, you may choose to eventually pursue paid speaking opportunities. Speaking fees vary widely depending on the industry and topic, and can range from $500 to $10,000 and up plus travel expenses. If you are interested in pursuing a career as a professional speaker, visit the National Speakers Association: www.nsaspeaker.org.

BOOK REVIEWS

Book reviews can be a wonderful way for an author to get exposure, though they are most commonly written for fiction books. Unless your nonfiction book is extremely unique (or you are a celebrity), it's unlikely that you are going to be able to get the attention of traditional book reviewers. However, there are many other ways to reel in reviews and exposure for your book.

1. Contact Writers Who Cover Your Subject Matter

Go directly to the source by reaching out to reporters who cover your topic. If you're an author of a business book, you should target reporters who cover business; a cookbook author should contact food writers; and an author of a sports guide should contact sports reporters. Don't waste your time—or the reporter's time—by reaching out to those who cover general news or topics that have nothing to do with your book.

Once you identify the writers who are most interested in your subject matter, reach out to them. Reporters need authors as much as we need them! They are always on the look-out for story ideas and sources to interview so don't be afraid to contact them via e-mail (most publications have websites that make it easy to locate and contact reporters).

I recommend sending a brief e-mail to introduce yourself and your book. Include a short synopsis (one or two paragraphs), a brief bio about you, and ask the reporter if he/she would like to receive a complimentary review copy. (Review copies are golden opportunities. Be willing to send these out often.)

Some reporters will turn you down. Some won't even respond. This is the reality of the publicity game. However, it's quite likely that you will end up in a database of sources. You could hear from them again down the road.

For those who do request that review copy, send it promptly along with a brief personal note of thanks. Be sure to follow up within a couple of weeks with an e-mail. Ask if the book arrived safely and if the reporter has any questions for you. This is a good reminder to them to follow-through.

2. Reach Out to Bloggers

Tim Ferriss, author of *The 4-Hour Workweek*, has publicly cited bloggers as the secret to his book's best-selling status. He contacted dozens of influential business bloggers prior to the release of his book and offered them complimentary copies. Top bloggers have loyal fans and when they recommend a book or any product or service, their readers pay attention. You can research and locate blogs that reach your target audience through www.technorati.com.

3. Solicit Reviews on Amazon

Reader reviews on Amazon are highly influential. It is important to solicit reviews without them all coming from your grandparents, aunts, third cousins and friends. Ask your clients to write reviews. If you receive an e-mail from a happy reader, ask them to write a review. Ask, ask, ask at every opportunity.

4. Leverage Your Blog and/or Website

When you hear from a reader, ask if you can have their permission to publish their review on your blog or website. Most will gladly agree and these kinds of reviews are fantastic credibility-builders.

5. Invite Reviews

Reach out through your e-mail list, social media networks, blog and any other venue you have at your disposal and ask for reviews. One author I know who writes niche books sent a request out to his mailing list and received eight rave reviews on Amazon before the end of the day.

ADDITIONAL PROMOTION TIPS

Update Online Profiles

Many sites allow you to post a bio with your public profile. Make sure you have several versions of your bio readily available in short, medium and long formats. This will not only prevent you from having to recreate it each time, but it will ensure that your message is consistent. Showcase your expertise in your subject matter, mention your book(s) and always include a link to your site and/or blog. I keep my bio document handy on my desktop so that I can open it and copy information quickly at any time.

Publish a Newsletter

Build loyal fans for life by publishing an interesting electronic newsletter with content related to your book(s). My first newsletter went out to a whopping eight people several years ago. Today it goes out to thousands of subscribers. Include a sign-up box on every page of your site. Get started with www. ConstantContact.com or www.iContact.com.

Form Online Partnerships

Find people who reach a similar target audience and look for ways to team up and promote each other. You can publish articles on each other's websites or newsletters, host an event or contest together or even share a blog. Be creative and pool your resources.

Leverage Social Media

Sites like LinkedIn.com, Facebook.com, Twitter.com and countless others are ripe for finding and building an audience. Create an interesting profile and get active in social networking communities. The biggest cost here will be in your time so spend it wisely and identify the best opportunities to expand your reach.

Participate in Online Groups and Forums

Find online communities where your target audience looms and make a name for yourself by sharing information. If you really want to stand out, start and lead your own group. Some good places to start are groups.yahoo.com/, Facebook Groups, LinkedIn Groups and www.Ning.com.

Host an Open House

Invite clients, prospects, alliance partners, family and friends to an open house, barbecue, customer appreciation day event or cocktail party and celebrate your book. Set up a table where you can sell and sign copies and take plenty of pictures to blog about the event later.

Conduct a Virtual Book Tour

Contact bloggers, teleseminar hosts, and Internet radio shows and let them know that you are available for interviews. Book tours are typically conducted over a period of time (2 weeks is about average). Cross-promote the event by posting announcements through your social media channels and blog.

Leverage Media Coverage

Many people wonder what to do AFTER landing media coverage. Always update your bio and the media page of your website to reflect any coverage you have received. If a story or clip is available online, include a link. As your list of appearances grows, the natural progression can ultimately lead to bigger and better media opportunities.

Donate Books

Pick some favorite charities and offer copies of your books for their libraries or as give-aways for their events. Exposure is always beneficial, but more importantly, it's just good karma.

---

*"First you're an unknown, then you write one book
and you move up to obscurity."*

Martin Myers

INTERVIEW PROFILE

Your Name: Caterina Rando
Business Name: Attract Clients with Ease
Website:
www.attractclientswithease.com
www.imagebusinesscoach.com
www.directsalescoaching.com
Book Title:

- Learn to Power Think, Chronicle Books

Synopsis of Your Book:

Learn to Power Think is a how to self-help book that combines inspiration and exercises that allows the reader to see what area they want to improve in and gives them ideas on how they can uplift their lives.

Description of Your Business:

We provide education, tools and resources that show, support and inspire entrepreneurs in building profitable and sustainable businesses.

How has being an author has directly impacted your business?

Being a co-author gave me major exposure through book distribution nationwide. Because Staples carried my book I was able to cultivate a sponsorship with Staples that included speaking at conferences and in store events.

Have you received any media exposure as a result of your book?

We received a lot of print media, Balance magazine, Latina magazine. I also was asked to write a 6 page article for Redbook as a result of the editor seeing my book. I also did several radio interviews.

What are some of your favorite marketing strategies for your business and your book?

Speaking, speaking and more speaking.

How would you business be different today if you hadn't authored a book?

I guess I assume I would be successful anyway. A book gives you more confidence, more credibility and opens more doors for you.

Knowing what you know today, is there anything that you would do differently?

Yes, focused more on speaking engagements and getting booked to speak at conferences. I would have not wasted my time with lots of book store events and only done a very select few. I also would have built ancillary coaching programs around my book.

Do you have any advice for entrepreneurs who want to write a book?

Your book should only be a part of your platform and your marketing mix. Selling books should be a lesser goal. Build additional lucrative goals around your book release.

What are your plans for the future?

I do plan to write another book.

Is there anything else you would like to add?

Start writing.

Part Five:
Social Media Marketing for Business and Books

"Opportunity is missed by most people because it is dressed in overalls and looks like work."

Thomas A. Edison

SOCIAL MEDIA CROWD BUILDING

Though I've been marketing online since 2003, like a lot of people, I was initially resistant to the social media frenzy. I'm already too busy and didn't want to get involved in anything that would potentially take up any more of my time. But once I started to investigate the possibilities, I quickly discovered the power that exists in social media.

This section focuses on what I call The Big Three: Facebook, LinkedIn and Twitter. These are currently the most active social networks for business and each brings its own unique value. I usually recommend that you engage all three for business—and I'll explain the reasons coming up—but at the very least I urge you to start with Facebook. There are simply too many users there waiting to hear from you and you are definitely missing opportunities if you don't hop aboard this fast-moving promotion vehicle.

What the Heck is Social Media and How Can it Benefit My Business?

In a nutshell, social media allows you to connect, communicate and share compelling content with your target audience.

All of the major social media sites provide the opportunity to search for users by keyword (i.e., by city or industry). It's relatively easy to find your potential clients and readers. The real challenge is in keeping them engaged.

Social Media Influence

As the newspaper industry continues to suffer a slow death, social media is becoming a prime resource for information. News on social networks can break and spread at lightning speed. I personally learned about the deaths of Michael Jackson and Ted Kennedy through the almost instantaneous posts on Twitter.

During the wildfires in southern California in 2008, the firefighters posted updates from the scene on Twitter. Many would argue that Barack Obama won the presidential election largely due to the viral marketing campaigns launched through social media sites.

It is almost frightening to think about the power that social media holds and how it is shaping a new world.

What Social Media Can Do for Your Business and Your Book:

- ✓ Build brand recognition
- ✓ Change brand perception
- ✓ Establish or showcase your expertise in your field
- ✓ Attract new clients and readers
- ✓ Generate repeat exposure with existing clients and prospects
- ✓ Promote products
- ✓ Promote services
- ✓ Promote events
- ✓ Reach your local community
- ✓ Reach the global community
- ✓ Set your business and book apart from competitors
- ✓ Create leverage for media opportunities, publishing contracts, corporate sponsorships, speaking engagements and more (a large network creates demand)
- ✓ Trigger a viral effect

Viral Marketing Defined

Viral marketing is contagious! When someone is compelled to share your message (forward an e-mail, video clip, or some other form of electronic communication) and this is replicated repeatedly, the message takes on a viral effect. When used for marketing purposes, a viral campaign can be incredibly powerful (though they are not easy to manufacture).

One example of viral marketing was when the TV show Britain's Got Talent featured a dowdy woman with a huge voice: Susan Boyle. The video of her knock-your-socks-off performance was posted to YouTube and downloaded millions of times. Boyle quickly became a fan favorite and was ushered to interviews all over the U.K. and U.S., including several appearances on The Today Show. This frenzy led to a record contract, even though she ultimately lost the talent competition. You can view the video here: http://www.youtube.com/watch?v=wnmbJzH93NU

HOW BUSINESSES ARE USING SOCIAL MEDIA

I could write an entire book full of business examples for social media. For now, I will share with you some of my favorite examples. This section is meant to get your ideas cooking and introduce you to the power of social media for business.

Victoria's Secret

If you want to see a great example of brand-building, look at the Victoria's Secret fan page on Facebook. This is clearly a brand with a loyal following. The company is engaging with readers, sharing news about upcoming events along with promotions and discounts, and promoting products. Victoria's Secret is also using its Facebook presence to drive traffic back to their "Pink Nation" website.

Note that retailers can often get away with excessive promotion as many shoppers connect with retailers on social networks in search of discounts. But most service-based businesses need to focus on sharing compelling content vs. selling. For example, if you're a business consultant who does nothing but promote your services, book and products, you will quickly lose the interest of your audience.

Honda Civic Owners Club (yes, really!)

Facebook has thousands of themed online groups that users can join. From New Moms in Baltimore to Foodies in France, there are a wide variety of groups for fun and business.

When I came across the Honda Civic Owners Club, I was intrigued. This is not a group launched by a Honda car owner; it is a group *targeted toward them*. The group is hosted by the owner of a Honda auto parts company. Pretty smart, don't you think?

Hosting a group can be a great way to connect with your target audience. Instead of blatantly promoting your business or your book, you serve as a resource for your audience. In the case of the Honda group, when a message board discussion is started by someone who is having car trouble, the group host can share helpful tips and mention, "By the way, we have this part in stock...."

See how this works?

CIO Magazine

LinkedIn also features groups and quite frankly, this is where the majority of the action happens on LinkedIn. Unlike Facebook, which attracts a broad range of users, LinkedIn is far more business focused. The groups here are often taken a bit more seriously.

This CIO Forum is hosted by *CIO Magazine*. It's a great way for the magazine to connect with its target audience of readers. It also provides a place for CIOs to network with each other online (an added benefit for them).

For businesses that want to target CIOs for sales, this group provides an opportunity to engage on the message boards and get known with your target audience. You should never join a social network simply to sell. But what you can do is start to demonstrate your expertise by sharing compelling information, answering questions on message boards and engaging with the online community.

Groups by Region

If your target customers are in your own backyard, you can locate groups by region (search by city name). On LinkedIn I found 275 groups for Sacramento, which provides ample opportunity for me to connect to people in my geographic community. Facebook also allows you to search by keyword.

I recently had a speaking engagement in the small bay area town of Pittsburg, California. At the time, I couldn't locate a single group for this town. For those targeting smaller communities, you may need to reach out to nearby metro areas or seize the opportunity and START a group for your town! Talk about a great way to blaze a trail.

@NYTimes

One of my favorite case studies on Twitter comes from the *New York Times*. As newspapers are consolidating and closing up across the nation, the *New York Times* quickly figured out how to leverage Twitter—they have one of the largest followings on all of Twitter.

When you follow @nytimes, you receive updates to news articles that link back to the site. You can bet that they are driving a lot of traffic online and increasing revenues with website ads vs. traditional print ads. This is a smart shift in the publishing industry and a way for this publication to thrive.

I also subscribe to news alerts via e-mail from the *New York Times*. The subject line of the messages always leads with their Twitter handle: @ nytimes. This helps with recognition and building their following as more and more users begin to engage with Twitter.

Any business that generates content can learn from this example. Whether articles, videos, white papers, blog posts or photos, you can use Twitter and the other social networks to promote content and drive traffic back to your site!

Comcast Cares?

This Twitter profile has marketers everywhere buzzing. Comcast, a cable company, has suffered from a poor reputation for service. In a ground-breaking move, the company launched a Twitter profile: @Comcastcares.

They have put a human face on the profile and he is responsible for responding to posts and sharing information (actually, they have several employees in charge of this Twitter profile, but just one face).

Instead of allowing nasty-grams to stack up on the profile (which is the case for many of the utility companies), "Frank" from Comcast responds to users directly. He opens support tickets and follows up on cases until they are resolved. Notice that Comcast is also following all users back (they have the same number of followers as they are following). This also shows that they are paying attention to customers.

Comcast is changing its brand perception through Twitter and turning disgruntled customers into loyal champions.

Now that you've got some ideas brewing, let's move on to The Big Three and how you can use them....

"The victory of success is half won when one gains the habit of setting goals and achieving them. Even the most tedious chore will become endurable as you parade through each day convinced that every task, no matter how menial or boring, brings you closer to fulfilling your dreams."

Og Mandino

FACEBOOK

Launched as a way for founder Mark Zuckerberg to connect with friends at Harvard, Facebook has exploded into the mainstream. With nearly 200 million users, and a million new members joining each week in the U.S. alone, people are paying attention.

One of the biggest benefits that social media platforms like Facebook provide is the ability to generate repeat exposure with the people in your network. Clients, peers, readers, and prospects can make up your network, and you can promote events, sales, special offers and more through your Facebook profile.

Not only is Facebook a tool for your business, but it can be fun to connect with old friends, family and coworkers. There is something about sharing an old grade school photo that can create an instant bond with those from your past. And keep in mind that even personal connections have the potential to become new clients or readers.

How it Works

Facebook was initially designed to function like an interactive online yearbook. You start by creating a free personal profile that includes a photo, a bio, your website link and other details. Next, you can search for people you know and send each a friend request. Once accepted, your friend can see your profile and you can see theirs.

Central to the whole system is the status update box on Facebook that asks, "What are you doing?" Here is where users can share brief updates about anything from what they had for lunch to where they are headed for their next meeting.

These status updates contribute to a running stream of content. When you view your home page on Facebook, you will see the status updates from those in your network. In addition to brief text-based messages, users can share photos, videos and links. It's a bit like being a voyeur into the lives of those you're connected to. You also have the opportunity to comment back on posts and begin to engage in online conversation.

Using Facebook for Business

When leveraging Facebook for business, instead of sharing mundane details like the flavor of your latte of the day or which kid is headed to soccer practice, you can share details about your business or tips related to your book. For example, you might share a link to a recent blog post or offer up a discount on a featured service.

Though these details may not matter much to your family and friends, they will matter to your customers and prospects. This is where things start to get interesting. As you build a following of people in your community, you have an opportunity to engage them in your business.

Ready to get started? Here are some ways to maximize Facebook:

Create a Powerful Profile

There is no cost to create a profile on Facebook and based on site policies, your profile must be tied to a human name, not a business name. Use the "About Me" section to describe your business and what you do.

In the "Information" box on your main profile page, you can feature links to your website, blog and other business resources. Be sure to include a professional photo so that others can recognize you online. (By the way, if you have a staff, you should instruct them on how to do this too as they can help you reach an even bigger audience!)

Build Your Contact List

Facebook is based on the concept of connecting with friends. You can send and receive friend requests and once accepted, your friend can view your profile and you can view theirs. To begin connecting with people that you know, you can import your contact database or you can search Facebook for individual people by name.

You can also view the friends list for each person you are connected to. As an example, once you have accepted a friend request from your peer, Mary, you can then view her list of friends. If you know any of Mary's friends (or you would like to know them), send a connection request.

Take this a step further by connecting with others in your community. You can search Facebook by city name or by industry-related keywords. With the search results, you will find related people, groups and fan pages. Though you may not know some of the people in the groups you join, you can still send a friend connection request along with a note: "We are both members of XYZ group and I would love to connect and learn more about what you do."

Not everyone will accept your requests, but those who do will contribute to your growing network. The goal is to build a targeted network of contacts comprised of your target audience.

Communicate with Wall Posts

Each Facebook member has a "wall" where "friends" can post messages. This is a great place to post a quick note to those in your friends list. In the business networking world, this is the technological equivalent of picking up the phone to say hello.

For example, if you are connected to a CEO who you saw at an event recently, you could post a note on her wall that says, "Loved your presentation at the XYZ event – thanks for the great ideas!"

Remember, a big key to success with social media is communication. Take time to engage with those in your network. This doesn't require a significant amount of time. If you have a few minutes between appointments, log on and get involved.

Update Your Status

At the top of your Facebook home page is a status box. When you post a status update, everyone in your friends list can see your update on their home page. Those using Facebook for social purposes might update their status to say, "Time to put the kids to bed." For business purposes, this is a place to share tips, promote events and boost sales.

Effective business updates could include:

✓ Consulting services on sale! Save 20% on all services through the end of the month.

✓ New blog post: How to Sell Your Business.

✓ Before and after photos from our latest makeover—you won't believe this hot grandma!

✓ Money Tip: The more you make, the more you should save.

Remember, the idea is to engage your target audience. If all you do is sell, sell, sell, you will quickly lose interest. Mix up your posts with interesting articles, photos, links to resources and quick tips.

Create Fan Pages

Because Facebook requires that a personal profile be designated to a human, not a business, they provide the ability to create fan pages. You can create a fan page for a business, product, book, author, speaker, celebrity or just about anything you want. It is a good idea to launch a fan page for your business (while maintaining your private online profile which you can choose to use for personal connections or you can use as an extra way to gain exposure). You may also create an author fan page, or continue to use your personal profile—it's your choice.

To create a fan page, scroll all the way down to the bottom of Facebook and click on "Advertising" (don't worry, it doesn't cost anything to set-up). Next, click on "Pages" at the top of the screen. You will find some helpful explanations about how pages work, along with a link that will allow you to create your page.

Pages function a lot like profiles. You can add links, events, discussion boards and other features that make them interactive. Facebook will also post updates from your fan pages back on your profile so others know about them. And instead of sending friend requests out, you can invite others to become a "fan" of your page. You will also have the ability to send messages to your fans, allowing you to cultivate a community online.

A fan page can be a great tool for building exposure. It has a less personal feeling than a profile, but that can work to your advantage since you are using it for business purposes.

Participate in Groups

Online groups allow you to network virtually with potential clients and peers. To access groups, start from your Facebook home page, view the list of applications and click on "Groups." You can browse through thousands of themed groups with topics ranging from business to politics and everything in between.

You can search groups by city name, theme or any type of keyword. Start by searching for nearby cities. Business-related groups are a good place to focus since you're representing a business and can connect with other business-minded people. There are also moms groups, support groups, and themed groups on just about anything you can imagine.

If you really want to maximize the potential with groups, consider starting one of your own. Once again, there is no cost to do this and the visibility can be great. For example, if you want to target working moms in your city, you could start a group for busy moms in Atlanta. You do not need to promote your business at every turn. Instead, softly share what you do and post an occasional special offer, but provide value for members by sharing interesting content and engaging with them in the online forum.

Manage Your Time

The biggest complaint most have about social media is that it takes a lot of time to manage. I recommend designating time in your day for Facebook activities. You can login once or twice a day to view messages and manage your connections. Just be careful not to let time get away from you (it's easy to do!). Also, remember that the more time you spend on Facebook, the more ways you will find to use it to your advantage. Be creative, show your personality and have some fun. That will all be reflected in your success.

Engage Your Staff

Your staff members can bring added exposure for your business on Facebook, though a word of caution here: you don't want them to do more harm than good! If you have young folks working for you who use their Facebook pages to share drunken photos or dirty jokes, you probably don't want them talking about your business. But if you have staff members who want to build their business network, by all means share these details with them and help them extend the reach of your business.

FACEBOOK APPLICATIONS

There are hundreds of free applications that you can add to enhance your Facebook profile. You can search Facebook by keyword to find applications. For example, type in "blog" in the search box, click on the Applications tab and you'll see dozens of choices for blog-related applications. Following are some of my favorites.

Blog RSS Feeder

Import your blog posts directly to your profile!

www.facebook.com/apps/application.php?id=5315590686

Networked Blogs

This allows you to feed your blog posts into a tab on your Facebook profile and also adds your blog to a large directory of blogs. I use both Networked Blogs and the Blog RSS Feeder above.

www.facebook.com/networkedblogs

Books

As an author, you can share favorite books and reviews via an extra tab on your profile—and of course include a link to your own book.

Living Social:

www.facebook.com/apps/application.php?id=48187595837&

or WeRead:

ww.facebook.com/apps/application.php?id=2406120893&

TWITTER

Twitter is fast becoming the place to be if you want to gain more exposure online. The Twitter user base is growing and the demographics are compelling. According to a report by comScore Media Metrix, the largest user base on Twitter as of February 2009 were people ages 45 to 54, followed by 25 to 34 year olds and then 35 to 44 year olds. Moral of the story: Twitter isn't just for kids.

Twitter is built around status updates (similar to those you add in Facebook and also known as micro-blogging). The biggest difference is that Twitter only allows you to post 140 characters at a time—or about one sentence. This forces your communication to be concise, to say the least.

Twitter profiles are also much simpler than Facebook. You have just a few sentences to describe who you are and you can include one link to your website. Instead of sending along a friend request and waiting for it to be accepted, you choose to "Follow" people on Twitter. Once you do, you will see all of that user's status updates on your home page.

In a perfect world, once you follow someone on Twitter, they will follow you back and monitor your posts as well. Many will also view your profile to find out more about who you are.

Know the Terminology

Twitter has a language all its own. Here's a quick overview:

Tweet: A brief message you post as your status update for your followers to see—up to 140 characters.

Twitter handle: Your Twitter username is also known as your handle. An "at" symbol, '@,' always precedes a Twitter handle, which makes it linkable on Twitter. For example, my Twitter handle is @bizauthor so if someone wants to send me a direct tweet, they begin the message with @bizauthor to route it to me. Here's an example:

From @jeffkorhan:

@bizauthor You survived the NSA convention. Any highlights to share?

Retweet (aka RT): When you forward a tweet from someone else to your followers, this is known as a retweet and should begin with RT so that followers know what you're doing:

From @SandyDfromNJ:

RT @bizauthor: Entrepreneur-Author Tip: Attend several industry conferences each year for learning, networking and fun. [Great advice!!]

Note: when you send a RT, include your comments in brackets at the end of the message to distinguish your comment from the retweeted message.

Direct Message (aka DM): This is a direct message that you send to someone's Twitter Inbox.

Hashtag (aka #): Placing a hashtag (a pound sign), '#,' in front of a word improves the word's track-ability in Twitter search as it converts the attached word into a link that produces immediate search results. For example, if you are giving away a free report, you might include #freereport in your tweet. When you or anyone clicks on #freereport, Twitter will take you to a list of recent search results with that keyword.

Thank you (aka TY or THX): An abbreviation for thank you is simply TY to THX. You'll find lots of words abbreviated because of the limited space for tweets.

Create a Twitter Account

When creating a user name for Twitter, use your personal name if you want to brand yourself. You might create a separate Twitter profile for your business name, though if your business and book all fall under the same umbrella, one ID should do the job. It is difficult to change this down the road so be thoughtful with this decision. And unlike Facebook where profiles can only be created for humans, Twitter allows users to create profiles for companies.

Set Up Your Profile

Write an interesting description and include your book title, website link and a personal photo. It's also a good idea to set up your wallpaper with something unique (the background of your Twitter page). Many graphic designers now create custom Twitter backgrounds for around $100 and this is a worthy investment to make a distinctive impression.

Start Following People You Know

Search for people from your rolodex and begin following them to get started. This is also a great way to begin getting comfortable with Twitter. Sit back and watch what others are doing and then slowly begin to join in.

Follow to Build a Following

One of the most effective ways to build your list of followers on Twitter is to start by following others. If they are experienced Twitter users, they will likely follow you back. Therefore, the more people you follow, the more followers you will potentially add to your network.

The key to success here is not simply to follow en masse. Ideally, you want to focus on following your target audience of potential clients, readers and alliance partners. Keep in mind that as you follow others, they will want to know more about you which means that many will view your profile. Some will even visit your website and will also view your past tweets. It's a great way to introduce yourself and make connections.

You can search Twitter by name or you can search by keyword: search.twitter. com/. Also search for people by industry keywords through top directories like Twellow.com and wefollow.com.

Pay Attention to Posts

Are you finding interesting articles and valuable information? From a marketing perspective, this is the greatest advantage of using Twitter. You can exchange useful information with those who follow you, and learn from those whom you are following. This is also a great way to learn how people are using Twitter successfully. Pay attention to what you like and don't like about how others are sharing information on Twitter.

Share Interesting Content

Twitter was designed as a tool to share what you are up to. While you can tweet about what you're having for lunch, it's really not relevant (and can be annoying). The goal for business purposes is to share interesting content. You want to be a resource for your followers so that they will pay attention to what you're up to and will want to learn more—which is quite similar to your status update strategy in Facebook.

Always keep your target audience in mind. What do they want to know? You can share your own content as well as content from others. For example, you might share a link to an interesting article from a magazine website or blog or an instructional video on YouTube. You can certainly share discounts and promotions, though these should be balanced with other content unless you are a retailer (retail businesses often gain followers because of the discounts they provide).

Most importantly, mix it up, keep it interesting and engage daily.

Here are some ideas for things to tweet about:

- ✓ Link to your blog posts.
- ✓ Link to other people's blog posts. (Use RSS feeds to pay attention to interesting blogs and share the results with your followers.)
- ✓ Link to articles (yours or other sources. Could be major media outlets like a magazine or newspaper or a lesser-known site as long as it's interesting.).
- ✓ Brief tips with links to additional information on your site (bring users

back to your site!).

✓ Brief tips without links (It's a good idea to occasionally share tips without links too—you don't want to appear to be selling, selling, selling.).

✓ Invites to upcoming events.

✓ Announcements about conferences you are attending.

✓ Announcements about speaking engagements you are conducting.

✓ Recommended products, resources or just about anything that your followers would enjoy.

✓ Free give-aways. Use Twitter as a tool for giving away a free report or a ticket to your event. Get creative! Here's a recent example from an author:

From @JoelComm:

Giving away a copy of Twitter Power today. Simply follow @JoelComm and RT to enter.

At the end of the day, Joel can search results of everyone who participated and randomly choose a winner. Some companies are using trivia questions to give away iTunes gift cards and other prizes. Or you may simply provide a link for a free download. I sent this out recently:

From @bizauthor:

Free report! 25 Ways to Leverage Your Non-Fiction Book for Fun and Profit bit.ly/4htEpd

✓ Make Follow Friday recommendations. This is a trendy and useful activity to participate in on Fridays. The goal here is to recommend people that you suggest others follow. Use a hashtag so that your recommendation is included in the search results (#FollowFriday or #FF if you're short on space). It's best if you can tell people WHY you recommend someone. Here's an example:

#FollowFriday: Sacramento-area women entrepreneurs who rock! @TimeTamer, @bizauthor, @clarestweets

✓ Send a tweet to someone you want to connect with. For example, if you're going to a conference and want to meet the main speaker, send them a tweet prior to the event:

@bizauthor: Looking forward to your presentation at the NSA

conference!

Make a List of Tweets

Save time by planning your tweets in advance. I find it helpful to periodically sit down and do a serious "brain dump" of quick tips. I keep these in a Word document called "Tweets." As I come up with new ideas, I either immediately post them to Twitter or I add them to my running list to post later. After I add a tweet, I change the text to bold so I can keep track of what I've already shared.

Schedule Tweets

To save time, you can pre-schedule tweets to post at set times during the week (or assign this task to an assistant). I recommend scheduling at least one tweet to post each day, if not more. I usually login on Monday morning and schedule one post per day for the week (details on how to do this are coming up). Then, as the week goes on, I log in periodically to monitor activity, share something new, reply to people and engage in conversation.

Also note that not everyone is looking at Twitter at the same time so though you may have plenty of followers, if they aren't online when you send a post, they may never know it was there. Some people repost their tweets again later in the day or rotate them through the week to be viewed at different times on different days.

Acknowledge Your Allies

It can be courteous to send a thank you message to someone who recommends you or retweets your posts. For example:

From @StevenSchlagel:
@bizauthor thanks for the RT this week!

As your list grows and your information is forwarded around, your thank you messages might look like this:

From @EarthLifeInst:
TY 4 all the TwtR LOVE! @youRthere @bizauthor @TwistedLizard @
EarthLifeInst @DorothyDalton @wefollowfriday @TCusack247

If you have a ton of followers and many people retweeting your posts (a great problem to have), you can skip this step or simply send out a *"Thanks to everyone for the RTs! Much appreciated!"*

Engage With Your Audience

Social media is a two-way conversation. When you share something interesting, others will click your link, retweet your post or reply back to you. Look for opportunities to engage in conversation. Reply to people whose posts you find interesting. Retweet often as your followers will appreciate useful information, and those whose posts you share will be grateful. The more you engage the more benefits you will see as a result.

Be Interesting!

Let your personality shine through. Humor is always a good way to attract people. Find ways to stand out from the crowd.

Be Careful

Twitter is a public forum and as your list grows, you really can't know who is watching. Don't mention that you're going on vacation (your house will be empty). Don't tell people where your kids go to school. Be cautious and aware. This is good advice <u>for all online communications</u> so use common sense when sharing details about your life.

LINKEDIN

LinkedIn is a business-focused social network. The vast majority of users here are using LinkedIn for some kind of business purpose such as job hunting, recruiting, marketing or selling. The best news about LinkedIn is that its user base has a high median income with some reports indicating an average of over $100k per year. It's a smaller network compared to the mammoth Facebook, but it's highly-targeted for reaching users who can afford your services!

The LinkedIn profile is similar to Facebook and is intended to be used by individuals (not businesses). The real action on LinkedIn happens in Groups. LinkedIn Groups are remarkably active, covering a wide variety of business-related topics and alumni groups. Once again, you can search for groups by keyword, such as a city name or industry.

When you connect with a user on LinkedIn, you are required to know them or be acquainted with them in some way. It's harder to build a large following here because LinkedIn makes you specify how you know someone when you send them a connection request and can require you to verify this by entering the user's e-mail address. But if you're participating in groups, you can use this for an introduction:

"We're both members of the New York Entrepreneurs Club and I'd like to add you to my network."

When you join groups on LinkedIn, sign up to receive a daily digest of message board discussions via e-mail. This allows you to quickly scan conversations to see if there is anything interesting that you want to comment on. When you post a comment on a group message board, all members can view your comment and may also choose to view your profile. You will often benefit from a nice spike in connection requests after posting something interesting on a group message board.

You can also import your contacts list into LinkedIn to find out who has profiles there, share status updates and view the contacts lists for those you are connected to. Though LinkedIn is not as socially-focused as Facebook and makes it a bit harder to interact, it's worthwhile to at least maintain a presence here.

SOCIAL MEDIA TIME MANAGEMENT

By far one of the biggest concerns about using social media is the amount of time it takes to manage. It does take some time to get started, get your profiles set up and begin building a following, but it doesn't have to be a full-time job. Studies have shown that most marketers using social media spend an average of one hour per day managing their networks. You can do this yourself, delegate it to a staff member or even hire a company that offers social media proxy services if necessary. However, I strongly encourage you to actively engage yourself if at all possible. Authenticity comes through on these networks.

Monitoring Twitter

Once you begin following a lot of people on Twitter, there will be a lot of status updates going on. Tweet Deck (tweetdeck.com) is an indispensable and free tool for monitoring activity on Twitter and Facebook, especially as your connection list grows. Create groups to track your favorite Tweeters and easily reply and retweet posts from the console.

Tweetdeck also integrates with Facebook so that you can create a column to view status updates on Facebook or post a message through Tweetdeck that gets posted to Twitter and Facebook. I couldn't manage Twitter without it and frequently use it during the day to reply and retweet messages on Twitter.

Link Your Profiles Together

One great way to save time and improve the overall effectiveness of your social media efforts is to link all of your profiles together. This allows you to send a single status update that you push to all of your social networks at once as well as schedule your updates. Here are the steps to set this up.

1. Ping.fm – Use ping.fm to post one status update and have it pushed to Twitter, Facebook, LinkedIn and numerous other platforms. Recommendation: set this up to post to Facebook and LinkedIn ONLY and then integrate it with Hootsuite to incorporate Twitter. Keep reading…

2. Hootsuite.com – One of the best features offered by Hootsuite is the ability to schedule your tweets—this is a huge time-saver! You can configure Hootsuite to work with Ping.fm and seamlessly update all of your social media profiles at once during scheduled intervals. You can also login to Hootsuite at any time to post an update that you want to go out to all of your networks immediately.

3. socialoomph.com – You will find lots of free features with Socialoomph, including the ability to schedule your posts to certain networks (which you won't need if you're using Hootsuite to post to all of your social networks at once). I use this service for the following:

- ✓ Send an automatic direct message (DM) response to new Twitter followers. This is somewhat controversial. Some Twitter enthusiasts hate automated DMs (I don't particularly like receiving them myself, but as you add a large number of contacts, it just makes the process easier and saves time). I do not recommend trying to sell anything here! My DM invites users to also connect on Facebook, which helps me add an average of 20 new Facebook connections per day:

  "Thanks so much for following! Want to connect on Facebook too? www.facebook.com/stephanie.chandler.bizauthor"

- ✓ Automatically follow anyone who follows you. It is courteous to follow anyone who follows you on Twitter. You can vet your own followers one-by-one by viewing each profile and deciding if you want to follow them back, but again, as your list grows, this becomes very time consuming. I automatically follow everyone back. If I later find that they are sending spam or anything offensive, I unfollow or block them using TweetDeck. And yes, unfortunately you will encounter spammers on Twitter.

- ✓ Create keyword alerts similar to Google Alerts. I set up Socialoomph to monitor keywords and phrases including my name, website URLs, book titles and phrases related to my target audience. I receive a daily e-mail with the results so I can keep track of who mentions me or topics I am interested in.

4. bit.ly/ - To shrink web links, use the free link shortening service from bit. ly (you only have 140 spaces in a tweet so long links should be condensed). Even better, this tool will track how many click-throughs your link received. So if you want to link to a new blog post, you can shorten the URL to save space

and then track the results and find out how many people clicked the link. Pay attention to the trends so you know how your audience is responding to your posts.

Sample Social Media Activity

Here is an example of what your week might look like when managing your social media presence.

Monday

> *"Writing is not necessarily something to be ashamed of, but do it in private and wash your hands afterwards."*
>
> Robert Heinlein

(The busiest day of the week due to weekend catch-up and scheduling for the week)

8:00AM: Login to Hootsuite and post one tweet per day for the next five days that will be pushed out to all of your social networks.

8:15AM: Login to Facebook to view and accept connection requests generated over the weekend. Next, check Facebook Inbox for messages and reply if necessary. Finally, scan Facebook home page for interesting posts from your network and reply or comment on a few that are interesting.

8:25AM: Login to LinkedIn to view and accept connection requests and check inbox for messages.

8:30AM: Check out Twitter activity on Tweetdeck. Reply to any messages sent to you or find an interesting post from someone else to retweet.

1:20PM: Since you have a few minutes between appointments, check out Tweetdeck to view messages and respond. Always look for something interesting to retweet or send out an interesting post with some other news from your day. If you have time, take a quick look at Facebook to see what's happening there.

3:40PM: With a few minutes to spare, repeat steps from above. Check Tweetdeck and Facebook for updates and find a reason to engage. Or if you have something new to share, login to Hootsuite and send an update out to all of your networks.

5:00PM: Take one last look at Tweetdeck before you end your workday.

Total Time Spent: 65 minutes

Tuesday

8:00AM: No need to login since you have a scheduled tweet going out!

9:50AM: You have a few minutes to spare so check Tweetdeck for updates and reply as needed.

1:15PM: You've added a new blog post. Login to Hootsuite and share the title and a link (shortened with bit.ly) with your networks.

3:50PM: Check out Tweetdeck and Facebook for comments and activity from your blog post link. Reply or send thanks to those who shared the information via retweet or commented on your post.

5:00PM: No time left in the day so you skip it and wait until tomorrow.

Total Time Spent: 20 minutes

Wednesday

8:00AM: No need to login since you have a scheduled tweet going out! But you have some time and didn't check at the end of the day yesterday so you login to Tweetdeck, Facebook and LinkedIn to catch up on activity.

9:45AM: You just learned about a fun local event that you know your clients will love so you login to Hootsuite and send it out to your networks.

2:30PM: You have a few minutes so you check Tweetdeck for updates. You decide to retweet two interesting posts from those you follow.

4:45PM: Last look at Tweetdeck and Facebook. Reply to a few messages from your Facebook Inbox.

Total Time Spent: 30 minutes

Wednesday Night

8:15PM: While watching CSI, you boot up your laptop and look for people to follow on Twitter. You login to www.Twellow.com to search for keywords. Later, you hop over to Facebook and search for local businesses to connect with. Simply being connected to them will attract followers who also want to connect with local people.

Total Time Spent: 1 hour, 15 minutes

Thursday

8:00AM: No need to login since you have a scheduled tweet going out!

11:15AM: Your newsletter is going out today with a special discount on services. You decide to send out a post announcing the discount and remind people to sign up for your newsletter on your site (sent though Hootsuite).

1:50PM: Check out Tweetdeck and discover that several people retweeted your announcement. Send them a quick thanks then hop over to Facebook to reply to comments. You also have some new connection requests so you accept those as well.

3:30PM: Your client just told you about a great resource for industry articles. You visit the site, find an interesting article and send it out via Hootsuite. Then you update your Tweets document with links to a few more articles that you will schedule to go out later.

5:00PM: You take one final look at Tweetdeck, Facebook and LinkedIn. Lots of activity today because of your posts. Time well spent.

Total Time Spent: 40 minutes

Friday

8:00AM: No need to login since you have a scheduled tweet going out! But you decide to participate in Follow Friday and recommend a few of your top clients.

10:20AM: You have several cancellations for appointments on Friday due to flu season so you send out an announcement that the first three people to retweet your post will receive a free copy of your e-book.

10:35AM: Send a follow-up announcement thanking everyone and announcing the winning recipients of your e-book.

12:40PM: You upload some interesting photos to your website and use Hootsuite to send a link to check them out.

2:00PM: You're leaving early so you skip further updates and head out.

Total Time Spent: 15 minutes

Social Media Success Round-up

✓ Engage with your audience. While you can automate some of your social media activity, remember to show that there is a human being behind your profile.

✓ Participate often. Some amount of activity on a daily basis is best for maximum exposure. Remember that not everyone views their networks at the same time. For best visibility, rotate activity throughout the day.

✓ Balance your content and sales activity. Most businesses (with the exception of retail) should follow the 90/10 rule: 90% useful content, 10% sales.

✓ As an author, remember that you are building your personal brand and showcasing your expertise. You might be surprised by who follows your posts. Last month I was interviewed for *Entrepreneur Magazine* because the reporter was following my posts on Twitter!

✓ Be unique. Figure out how to set your business apart from your competitors. You can do this by being a resource for your community, sharing interesting content, holding contests, co-promoting with other businesses and building loyalty.

✓ Have a goal for your brand. What do you want to be known for? Who do you want to connect with? Be clear with your messaging.

✓ Add your Twitter, Facebook and LinkedIn profile links to your website and blog for maximum visibility. Links should be embedded in logos and featured in prime real estate on your website (like on the top of the sidebar across your entire site). This makes it easy for site visitors to connect with you.

✓ Promote your profile links in your e-mail signature, in your electronic newsletter, online profiles and anywhere you have online visibility.

✓ Connect with the people you want following you. In other words, seek out your target audience. Follow them on Twitter, reach out to them on Facebook and locate groups on LinkedIn where they congregate. Spend a minimum of one hour each week building your network.

✓ Pay attention to how others are using social media. This is an evolving medium. Look for what you like and don't like about how others are using their networks.

Always be on the lookout for ways to grow and stand out. Most importantly, <u>do what feels right to you</u>! There are a lot of people giving advice on this subject. You can learn from lots of sources and then pick and choose which advice makes sense to you.

INTERVIEW PROFILE

Your Name: Alexis Martin Neely
Business Name: Family Wealth Planning Institute
Website:
www.familywealthmatters.com
www.wearcleanunderwearbook.com
Book Title:

- Wear Clean Underwear, a Fast, Fun, Friendly-- and Essential-- Guide to Legal Planning for Busy Parents

Description of Your Business:

The Family Wealth Planning Institute makes it possible for families and small business owners to have affordable access to a lifetime relationship with a lawyer.

How has being an author has directly impacted your business?

The book has directly impacted my business by serving as a lead generation piece for my own law firm before I sold it, and now for the lawyers I train throughout the United States. When prospects read it, they come in ready to engage our services. It has also opened the door to media coverage for me.

What kind of media exposure have you received as a result of your book?

Yes, as a result of publishing the book, I have been featured on the Today Show, Better TV and CNBC as a regular legal commentator and many radio programs and other local television.

What are some of your favorite marketing strategies for your business and your book?

I offer the first chapter of the book as a free download to entice people to read the rest. My most favorite marketing is direct response marketing in which I give away something for free, like my book, in exchange for contact information and then I develop a relationship through my regular weekly e-mail newsletter.

How would you business be different today if you hadn't authored a book?

The credibility factor of being an "author" would not be there and the media appearances probably wouldn't have come so easily without the book. I also would not be seen as the expert in my field without the book.

Knowing what you know today, is there anything that you would do differently?

I would have written the book sooner!

Do you have any advice for entrepreneurs who want to write a book?

Do whatever you need to do get it done—if you are too busy or don't know what to say, hire someone to do it or get someone to coach it out of you. The book is so vital to talking your business to the next level that you just need to hunker down and get it done—no matter what it takes!

What are your plans for the future?

I plan to keep changing the way the way the American public thinks about lawyers and to spread my message about living life on your own terms to millions of people across the globe. I see a TV show and many more books in my future.

Resources

"I am always doing that which I cannot do, in order that I may learn how to do it."

Pablo Picasso

Books for Writers

- ✓ *Bird by Bird* by Anne Lamott

- ✓ Jump Start Your Book Sales by Tom and Marilyn Ross

- ✓ 1001 Ways to Market Your Books by John Kremer

- ✓ Beyond the Bookstore: How to Sell More Books Profitably to Non-Bookstore Markets by Brian Jud

- ✓ The Self-Publishing Manual by Dan Poynter

- ✓ How to Write a Book Proposal by Michael Larsen

- ✓ Write the Perfect Book Proposal: 10 Proposals That Sold and Why by Jeff Herman and Deborah M. Adams

- ✓ Guerrilla Marketing for Writers: 100 Weapons to Help You Sell Your Work by Jay Conrad Levinson, Michael Larsen, and Rick Frishman

- ✓ *Writer's Market* by Kathryn S. Brogan

- ✓ Jeff Herman's Book of Publishers, Editors, and Literary Agents by Jeff Herman

- ✓ The Author's Guide to Building an Online Platform: Leveraging the Internet to Sell More Books by Stephanie Chandler

- ✓ From Entrepreneur to Infopreneur: Make Money with Books, eBooks and Information Products by Stephanie Chandler

Various Resources for Writers

✓ Publisher's Marketplace provides publishing industry news and resources for publishers, editors, and agents: www. publishersmarketplace.com/.

✓ Para Publishing is Dan Poynter's site for self-publishers. His weekly newsletter is loaded with tips and information: www.parapublishing. com.

✓ Writers Market is a subscription-based service from the folks at Writer's Digest that allows you to search for market information for consumer and trade magazines, newspapers, and literary agents: www.writersmarket.com/.

MAGAZINES FOR WRITERS

✓ *Writers Digest*: www.writersdigest.com/

✓ *The Writer*: www.writermag.com/

✓ *Poets & Writers Magazine*: www.pw.org/

✓ *Publisher's Weekly* is a print magazine and website that is a staple in the publishing industry for learning about trends in the marketplace: www.publishersweekly.com/. Because the subscription price is hefty, you may want to read this one at your local library. There is no charge to subscribe to their e-zine.

GROUPS AND ASSOCIATIONS

- ✓ Entrepreneur-Authors Group on Facebook:
  www.entrepreneur-authors.com
- ✓ The Independent Book Publishers Association:
  www.ibpa-online.com
- ✓ Small Publisher's Association of North America:
  www.spannet.org
- ✓ Small Publishers, Artists, and Writers Network:
  www.spawn.org/
- ✓ American Society of Journalists and Authors:
  www.asja.org

RESOURCES FOR FINDING AGENTS

✓ The Association of Authors' Representatives is a member-based organization for agents who follow a code of conduct. www.aar-online.org

✓ Publisher's Marketplace offers a directory of agents. www.publishersmarketplace.com/

✓ Predators and Editors is an online directory of literary agents, including warnings about agents who aren't reputable. www.anotherealm.com/prededitors/.

✓ Go to the bookstore or library to check out books in your genre. Most authors give a special thanks to their agent in the acknowledgements section.

RESOURCES FOR SPEAKERS

- ✓ www.SpeakerLeads.com – Directory of associations and events in need of speakers
- ✓ SpeakerNetNews.com – Great free newsletter with subscriber tips for all-things-speaking
- ✓ www.sharingideasmag.com – Recently re-launched, online magazine for speakers, which was originally published by Dottie Walters
- ✓ www.antion.com/ - Tom Antion provides tips for breaking in to professional speaking

TRADE ASSOCIATIONS

✓ www.nsaspeaker.org/ - National Speakers' Association

✓ www.astd.org/ - American Society for Training and Development

✓ www.asla.com/ - American Seminar Leaders Association

✓ www.toastmasters.org/ - Toastmasters is a resource for developing and refining your skills as a speaker, with chapters all over the country.

LinkedIn Groups

- ✓ www.linkedin.com/groups?gid=2950959 - Nonfiction Authors
- ✓ www.linkedin.com/groups?gid=48422 – ASTD National
- ✓ www.linkedin.com/groups?gid=125470 – Global Keynote Speakers Association
- ✓ www.linkedin.com/groups?gid=1742397 – Need a Speaker/Be a Speaker
- ✓ www.linkedin.com/groups?gid=37544 – Professional Speakers and Seminar Leaders

BOOKS FOR SPEAKERS

- ✓ *Speak and Grow Rich* by Dottie Walters and Lilly Walters

- ✓ *The Wealthy Speaker* by Jane Atkinson

- ✓ *1001 Ways to Make More Money as a Speaker, Consultant or Trainer* by Lilly Walters

- ✓ *Getting Started in Speaking, Training or Seminar Consulting* by Robert W. Bly

- ✓ *Money Talks: How to Make a Million as a Speaker* by Alan Weiss

- ✓ *How to Make it Big in the Seminar Business* by Paul Karasik

- ✓ *Secrets of Successful Speakers* by Lilly Walters

ABOUT THE AUTHOR

Stephanie Chandler is an author of several business and marketing books:

- LEAP! 101 Ways to Grow Your Business (Career Press)

- From Entrepreneur to Infopreneur: Make Money with Books, eBooks and Information Products (John Wiley & Sons)

- The Author's Guide to Building an Online Platform: Leveraging the Internet to Sell More Books (Quill Driver Books)

- The Business Startup Checklist and Planning Guide (Aventine)

Stephanie is also the founder and CEO of Authority Publishing, which provides custom book publishing and Internet marketing services. A frequent speaker at business events and on the radio, Stephanie has been featured in *Entrepreneur Magazine*, *BusinessWeek*, Inc.com, *Wired Magazine* and many other media outlets.

Visit Stephanie Chandler's Sites:

- ✓ Custom Book Publishing: www.AuthorityPublishing.com
- ✓ Author & Speaker Information: www.StephanieChandler.com
- ✓ Resources for Entrepreneurs: www.BusinessInfoGuide.com
- ✓ Nonfiction Writers Conference:
  www.NonfictionWritersConference.com

Social Media:

- ✓ Twitter: twitter.com/bizauthor
- ✓ Facebook: www.facebook.com/stephanie.chandler.bizauthor
- ✓ LinkedIn: www.linkedin.com/in/stephaniechandler

CPSIA information can be obtained at www.ICGtesting.com
Printed in the USA
BVOW012239231011

274357BV00005B/5/P

9 781935 953043